WICCA FOR BEGINNERS

A Guide to the Wiccan Beliefs, Rituals, Magic, and Witchcraft

BY LISA CHAMBERLAIN

Wicca for Beginners

Published by **Occult Shorts**

ISBN: 1503008223

ISBN-13: 978-1503008229

Disclaimer

No part of this publication may be reproduced or transmitted in any form or by any means, mechanical or electronic, including photocopying or recording, or by any information storage and retrieval system, or transmitted by email without permission in writing from the publisher.

While all attempts have been made to verify the information provided in this publication, neither the author nor the publisher assumes any responsibility for errors, omissions, or contrary interpretations of the subject matter herein.

This book is for entertainment purposes only. The views expressed are those of the author alone, and should not be taken as expert instruction or commands. The reader is responsible for his or her own actions.

Adherence to all applicable laws and regulations, including international, federal, state, and local governing professional licensing, business practices, advertising, and all other aspects of doing business in the US, Canada, or any other jurisdiction is the sole responsibility of the purchaser or reader.

Neither the author nor the publisher assumes any responsibility or liability whatsoever on the behalf of the purchaser or reader of these materials.

Any perceived slight of any individual or organization is purely unintentional.

YOUR FREE GIFT

As a way of showing my appreciation for purchasing my book, I'm giving away an exclusive, free eBook to my readers—*Wicca: Little Book of Wiccan Spells*.

The book is ideal for any Wiccans who want to start practicing magic. It contains a collection of ten spells that I have deemed suitable for beginners.

You can download it by visiting:

www.wiccaliving.com/bonus

I hope you enjoy it.

CONTENTS

INTRODUCTION

If you're reading this book, you probably already know that Witches and Wiccans are *real* people, living in the contemporary world—not the mean, green-faced, scary old hags seen in popular movies and Halloween costumes.

They are not malicious, and they don't hex people or try to manipulate anyone through devious means.

Although many Wiccans and Witches may be secretive about their work and faith, there is nothing sinister about what they do. These stereotypes resulted from misconceptions about older, pagan religions found throughout Europe before the rise of Christianity, and while they may provide for good entertainment, they have also obscured the truth.

This has, unfortunately, prevented many people from knowing anything about the rich beauty of the traditions and the positive experiences for those following this spiritual way of life. Happily, you will soon know more about the realities, rather than the myths about Wicca.

In fact, interest in Wicca, Witchcraft, and contemporary magic has increased exponentially over the past few decades. This is at least in part thanks to the Internet. Just twenty years ago, people curious about these subjects might have had very little access to credible information, especially those without a good New Age or Occult bookstore anywhere in the vicinity. The internet has made information available to anyone who seeks it. Not every website is of equal quality, of course, and people are advised to disregard anything that doesn't "feel" right for them. This is true for print sources, as well.

No matter where you find your resources, you'll find that the more widely you read, the more varied the definitions, terminology, and even philosophy and beliefs involved in Wicca and Witchcraft become, as people writing on the subject come from a multitude of traditions and perspectives on the Craft. Wiccan authors can sometimes be an argumentative bunch—as people passionate about any religion can be—and you might find that some sources resonate with you more than others. Since there is no single authoritative source on the subject, it's up to you to choose whatever ideas and practices make the most sense to you.

This guide is intended as a brief introduction to the subject, covering the most basic questions that people curious about Wicca tend to have.

We'll be exploring the religion of Wicca, the history of its modern origins, and the basic beliefs systems that its various traditions hold in common. Then, we'll move on to magic, as we look at common Wiccan practices, including the relationship between Witchcraft and magic, and covering some of the common tools and rituals involved. Finally, I'll provide additional insights for those interested in learning more, borrowing from my own experience as a practicing Wiccan, and providing you with a sample ritual and spell suitable for a beginner, for those of you looking to practice magic.

Of course, no one guide can ever do a topic as diverse as Wicca justice, especially as every Wiccan has their own personal set of opinions and beliefs. For those of you wanting to learn more, I'll end this guide by suggesting several other points of reference for further reading, as well as sample tables of correspondence identifying the magical properties of selected colors, crystals, herbs and oils for you to experiment with, if you wish.

By the end of the book you will have a solid sense for the basics of Wicca and Witchcraft, and, I hope, a stronger desire to pursue this path.

Blessed Be.

SECTION ONE

INTRODUCTION TO WICCA

WHAT *IS* WICCA?

Before we get started, it's well worth establishing what Wicca really *is*.

Wicca is classified as a nature-based religion encompassing a wide variety of beliefs, traditions and practices inspired by many different sources—Wiccans often refer to these sources as "the Old Religion."

There are several different forms and traditions under the umbrella term of "Wicca," generally with overlapping elements such as pantheism, polytheism, an emphasis on ritual, and a deep respect for all living things.

Wicca has been described as a shamanic religion. "Shamanism" is a term originally used to refer to ancient religions found in regions of Asia, but it has since been used in reference to many indigenous traditions throughout the world, whose origins predate written history. Shamanism is often called the world's first religion, although it would not have looked like the major religions of today with their uniform beliefs and consistent practices that span continents.

Characteristics of shamanic traditions include an animistic world view, using altered states of consciousness to interact with the spirit world, and using the knowledge found there for healing and general well-being of the community. Shamans were the first "medicine people" and were revered in their societies. Like shamans, Wiccans seek connection with the unseen spirits of nature and work with natural agents such as stones and herbs for healing and protection.

Wicca is also considered to be a Pagan religion. Like "shamanism," "paganism" is also an umbrella term. It has been defined in the broadest sense as any religion that isn't Christianity, Judaism, or Islam, but it's more accurate to say that paganism involves nature-based belief systems that often (but not always) include several deities.

The word "pagan" comes from the Latin, where it meant "country person," and didn't have any religious association. Later, the word took on a negative connotation when Christianity tried to stamp out the old beliefs and practices of the country dwellers in Europe and other places it sought to dominate.

As a nature-based collection of beliefs and practices, Wicca is a type of paganism, but there are many other modern Pagan traditions besides Wicca. Some Wiccans resist the term and draw a clear distinction between themselves and Pagans. However, this distinction is aimed more at modern (or "Neopagan") spiritual movements than the general sense of the word as a category of "religion." What Neopagan traditions, Wiccan and non-Wiccan alike, have in common is an affinity with older, pre-Christian belief systems that may not be well-represented in written history but have retained a place in the human imagination, even if their particular expressions have morphed and changed over time. "The Old Religion" isn't found in a particular text or place or culture, but is a sort of catch-all name for the various strands of older cultural and spiritual beliefs that inform today's practices.

While it claims spiritual roots in older shamanic and pagan belief systems, Wicca itself is a *modern* religion, of relatively recent origins, and the use of the word "Wicca" as an official name for the religion came about several years after its initial founding. Since there is no consensus on any particular text, practice, or specific belief, there is a lot of leeway in terms of who might "claim" to be Wiccan, though many practices overlap among different traditions, groups, and individuals.

Among the many aspects of Wicca that distinguish it from other, more widely recognized religions is its emphasis on the feminine, as symbolized by nature, the Earth, the Moon, and feminine deities (or goddesses). The masculine is also represented through deity and is particularly associated with the Sun, but there is none of the patriarchy often found in other Western faiths.

Belief systems and practices identifying as Wiccan *can* be highly formalized and include hierarchical structures within practicing groups, but can also be very individualized and "free-form." The oldest forms of modern Wicca began with elaborately ritualized practice and hierarchical structures through which some Witches would rise through degrees of initiation to become High Priestesses and Priests.

Some covens today closely follow these original forms, while others have adapted and invented new forms, including more egalitarian structures. Some covens are for women only, while others are open to men and women. There are also an untold number of solitary Witches who prefer to practice alone. Some identify as eclectic, meaning that they don't follow any pre-existing tradition, but draw from many sources.

Wicca's modern history is full of interesting and unusual characters whose various contributions to the practice are a subject of much study and debate by today's historians of the movement. But before delving into the key points of Wicca's origins, let's look at some of the terms often associated with the name "Wicca."

Is Wicca *really* a religion?

In a word: Yes!

Although it is far less organized and visible than other faiths such as Judaism, Christianity, or Islam, Wicca has been recognized as being entitled to the same religious protections by courts in the United States, and is even included in the chaplain's handbook of the U.S. Army. In the UK, Wiccan priests and priestesses are authorized to function as prison chaplains, but Wicca is not officially recognized as a religion.

Wicca is sometimes referred to by those outside the practice as a "cult," possibly because it's called one in the Oxford English Dictionary. But this word is also tricky. "Cult" has several, neutral meanings, though unfortunately for Wiccans, it's often associated with negative images and groups with charismatic leaders like the followers of Jim Jones. Regardless, "cult" is not generally used by Wiccans to describe Wicca.

Most authors on the subject refer to Wicca as a religion, particularly those who identify as Wiccans. However, others who use the terms "Wicca" or "Wiccan" to describe their beliefs and practices don't necessarily regard Wicca as a religion that they follow or "belong to." This may be because Wicca has no central text, prophet, or other source of authority like the dominant Western religions, and its structures and forms of worship vary extremely widely. It may also be because the word "religion" has associations that some Wiccans are not comfortable with. (Many people in general will describe themselves as "spiritual" rather than "religious," and there's no shortage of Witches who do the same.)

For various reasons, the number of people identifying as Wiccans in predominately English-speaking countries is harder to accurately estimate than it is for more dominant religions. Many choose not to disclose their religion in a culture where it is not respected and is often enough even hostilely opposed. Others who might openly identify as Wiccans are uncounted, as there are no official houses of worship for them to be members of.

Nonetheless, some scholars reviewing random phone surveys over the past few decades have estimated that close to one million people around the world consider themselves Wiccans, with the majority found in the U.S. and the U.K. Whatever the actual count might be, it's clear that the numbers are rising steadily in the 21st century, as more knowledge about the religion becomes available and widely shared.

What's the difference between a Witch and a Wiccan?

Depending on who you ask, there's a big difference, or there's not much (if any) difference.

In terms of language, the words "witch" and "wicca" are related, as "wicca" was the Old English word that later became "witch."

However, among Wiccans the relationship between the two words is less black-and-white—there are Witches who identify as Wiccans, Witches who don't, and Witches who don't have a preference. There are also Wiccans who don't identify as Witches.

The varied uses of these words can be seen throughout contemporary writing about Wicca and Witchcraft. In addition to the name of the religion, some authors use "Wicca" as a singular word in place of "Witch," but most use "Wicca" as a plural term, meaning that several (or all) Wiccans can be collectively called "the Wicca."

Finally, while the words "Wicca" and "Wiccan" tend to be capitalized—especially in reference to the religion and its members—but there seem to be no hard and fast rules regarding whether to capitalize the words "Witch" and "Witchcraft" or leave them in lower case.

Some followers of Wiccan traditions who don't adopt the name "Wicca" as a personal identifier feel no need to identify with a capital "W" for "Witch" or "Witchcraft." Others feel that capitalization of these terms is important in distinguishing Wicca as an official religion and establishing a cultural respect for it as such. In the spirit of respect for those who feel strongly about recognizing Wicca as a religion, this guide capitalizes all four terms.

What's the difference between Wicca and Witchcraft?

Wiccans who don't identify as Witches don't use the term "Witchcraft" in association with their practice of Wicca—they don't use magic, and they draw a distinction between Wicca as a spiritual practice and individual relationship with the divine, and witchcraft as a practice that is not necessarily spiritual.

However, many Wiccans do blend magic into their practice to varying degrees, and may use "magic" as an interchangeable term with "Witchcraft" (often shortened to "the Craft") in association with Wicca.

In fact, some Witches who practice Witchcraft don't identify as Wiccan at all.

What does Wicca have to do with magic?

Once again, it depends on who you ask, and for Wiccans who don't practice magic of any kind, the answer is probably "nothing." However many, many Wiccans *do* include magic in their practice, to the point that the two are combined in many Wiccan books and resources—including this very guide!

Most Witches will refer to their practice of magic as Witchcraft, but may use either term. And of course, the word "magic" is also a bit tricky, as it has its own set of meanings.

"Ceremonial magic" is older than Wicca and was an original influence for what would eventually become Wicca, but it's actually a practice in its own right—in other words, not part of the religion. This ceremonial magic has several differences from the magic practiced by Witches. Ceremonial magic was derived from occult traditions through secret societies like the Freemasons and the Hermetic Order of the Golden Dawn, and is often quite elaborately ritualized. The term "high magic" is sometimes used to distinguish it from Witchcraft, which is called "folk magic" or even "low magic" by many of its practitioners. Some who practice ceremonial magic may identify as Pagans but are not Wiccans or Witches. Some simply identify as magicians.

What some call "practical magic" is a kind of ceremonial magic aimed at achieving common life improvements, such as healing physical or emotional ills, attracting love, and improving one's finances. Some Wiccans see this form of magic as non-spiritual and distinct from Wicca, but others blend the two by performing magic in alignment with their deities and for the good of all, rather than just for their own personal gain.

THE KNOWN HISTORY

The modern origins of Wicca can be traced back to the British Occult movement in the late 19th century.

A few key figures credited with developing and advancing Wicca as a religion are Gerald Gardner, Cecil Williamson, Patricia Crowther, and Lois Bourne. Gardner (1884-1964) is widely credited as being the founder of Wicca, although he and his fellow witches didn't use the term "Wicca" as an identifying term, but rather called their practice "Witchcraft," (sometimes shortened to just "the Craft") or "the Old Religion." Gardner did refer to the members of his tradition as "The Wica," but "Wicca" as a name for the religion was not used regularly until the 1960s as it spread to the U.S. and Australia.

Gardner had become interested in a theory advanced in the early 1920s by anthropologist Margaret Murray (1863-1963), which held that a pagan religion with a lineage going back to ancient times had existed in secret throughout the rise and domination of Christianity in Western Europe. Murray called this religion a "witch cult" and asserted that its practitioners were organized into 13-member groups, or covens, and worshipped a male "horned" god.

In the early 1940s, Gardner's exploration of mystical and occult experiences inspired him to develop a new incarnation of the witch cult, and he formed the Bricket Wood coven. Blending ideas from Murray with other sources such as Freemasonry, ceremonial magic, and the work of other Occult authors, Gardner's tradition expanded the deity worship to include a female goddess element along with the male god.

In 1947, Gardner met and befriended Aleister Crowley (1875-1947), a well-known occultist and writer who had explored and participated in a wide variety of religious and esoteric traditions from around the world, including Buddhism, Jewish mysticism, Hinduism, the Tarot, astrology, and more. Crowley's writings had a significant influence on Gardner, who included some of the rituals devised by Crowley in his own work. It was Crowley who coined the spelling of "magick" with a "k," to distinguish his form of magic from other "ceremonial magic"—and even stage magic—practices of the time.

Crowley is a complicated figure for many Wiccans today. Some of the practices he engaged in were considered to be scandalous, and his part in the history of the religion helped perpetuate an incorrect association between Wicca/Witchcraft and Satanism.

It should be noted here that "Satanism" is part of the Christian world view and not a pagan concept, and that Wicca does not, and never did, incorporate, endorse, or practice "Satanism" or the worship of anything "evil."

Furthermore, Crowley had a reputation for being misogynist and racist, which are attitudes incompatible with the Wiccan way of life.

At any rate, the tradition now known as Gardnerian Wicca began to flourish as Gardner brought other interested Occultists into his coven, including several women, one of whom was Doreen Valiente (1922-1999). Valiente became the High Priestess of Bricket Wood in the early 1950s and revised much of the original material the coven had been using, in part because she felt it had too much of Crowley's influence. Eventually, Valiente parted ways with Gardner over what she felt to be his irresponsible attempts to make modern Witchcraft known to the masses, and his decision to limit the power of women in the coven in response to their criticisms.

Valiente formed her own coven in 1957, and went on to study Witchcraft with other leading figures in the movement, ultimately writing several influential books that helped launch the evolution of Witchcraft from a secret society phenomenon to a widespread, highly individualized practice. Other leading figures in the expansion of the Craft were Alex Sanders (1926-1988), who founded the Alexandrian tradition of Wicca, and Raymond Buckland, who formed the Seax-Wica tradition in the early 1970s. Born in 1934, Buckland is credited with bringing Gardnerian Wicca to the United States, and has written dozens of books on Witchcraft and other esoteric subjects.

It was during the second half of the 20th century that what is collectively called Wicca spread from England to the rest of the United Kingdom, and to the United States and Australia, branching out into several different traditions. While those who follow the Gardnerian traditions and its direct offshoots often draw a distinction between Wicca and other, non-Wiccan witchcraft, many people identify as Wiccans regardless of the origins of their particular practice. These include people following Dianic, Celtic, and Georgian traditions, as well as "eclectic" practices adapted from a range of traditions.

"Claiming" the Wiccan identity

One particular distinction often drawn between followers of Gardnerian and Gardnerian-inspired traditions and other kinds of Witches is the concept of "lineage." Gardner, who claimed to have received much of the knowledge he based his coven's work on from "ancient sources," performed rituals of initiation to formally admit new people to the secrets of the Craft, much like the Freemasons and other occult orders.

As Gardnerian Wicca grew and evolved, members of the Bricket Wood coven went on to form other covens and initiated new witches into the tradition. This practice was adopted by other off-shoots of Gardnerian Wicca, as well, so that today's Gardnerian (or Alexandrian, etc.) Witches can generally trace their initiatory "lineage" back to the early origins of Wicca.

As information and new ideas about Witchcraft spread, however, the requirements of initiation and lineage became less "absolute," and the options of self-initiation and solitary practice became popular for people who were interested in the Craft, but were unable (or unwilling) to join or start a coven. Solitary Witches may follow a specific tradition closely, or may create their own versions of Wicca from a number of sources, and may or may not even call themselves Wiccan. Many prefer the term "eclectic Witch" as a way of describing their "DIY" approach to Witchcraft, but even eclectics are likely to involve at least some elements of the more formal traditions of Wicca in their practice.

While it may seem to some that solitary or eclectic Witches can't be true "Wiccans" if they don't follow the set practices of Wicca as laid out by its initial founders, the flexibility and adaptability that draws so many to the religion was actually part of its inception. Gardner's original material was based on a combination of other, pre-existing sources, and was revised and added to throughout his own time. He was observed to have told his own followers that they should treat the Book of Shadows (his name for the collected material used in ritual and magical practice) not as a permanent text, but as something to add to and alter for themselves as they saw fit.

So there really is no true "doctrine" of Wicca to follow, and no way to truly "claim" the name at the exclusion of others, whether one is solitary or participating in a "lineage" tradition.

THE UNKNOWN HISTORY

Despite the claims of Margaret Murray, Gardner, and others to have discovered and revived an authentic ancient tradition, academic historians never could find much factual evidence to support the "witch-cult" theory. And within the movement, leaders' claims of trance states, being "descendants" of ancient Witch lineages or "reincarnations" of Witches from former centuries were sometimes doubted, even by other Witches.

It's possible that anxiety over the perceived degree of validity and authenticity of Wicca has caused some Witches to take strong stances in favor of one tradition over others, one belief over another, and to argue incessantly about it. It's also possible that these questions of authenticity led some Witches to draw more heavily from what is known about traditions from other cultures and other esoteric practices than from the specific material that was supposed to link the modern religion directly to its ancient past.

Yet, with all that is unknown about the past peoples and cultures that Wicca draws inspiration from, what *is* known is that there was *something*, some energetic phenomenon that was mystical and magical enough to keep a hold on humanity, even through the rise of Christianity and its eventual domination of the parts of the world most frequently associated with the "Old Religion." European folk magic traditions, many of which are incorporated into Wiccan magic, were possibly descended from this same source. And we also know that pagans and shamans of cultures around the world sought to interact with the unseen world in similar ways, through music, dance, and altered states of consciousness.

So it might be enough to say that what the original founders of modern Wicca did was create new forms through which people could tap into the mystical, bridging the gap between the ancient and modern worlds with new expressions of a magical energy that has always existed. There may be a dizzying variety of interpretations of these new forms, but there are enough commonalities among them, and enough people participating, to make it clear the "Old Religion" is back, and here to stay.

WHAT DO WICCANS BELIEVE?

Imagine an existence before "modern civilization" as we know it.

There is no electricity, no running water, no telephone communication, and no Internet (gasp!). You can't get tropical fruits in a supermarket in January even though you live thousands of miles from the nearest banana farm. There are no books, magazines, or newspapers. No weather forecasts, no news bulletins or alarms to warn of tornadoes, blizzards, or hurricanes. No calendars to mark the passing of the months, and no clocks to mark the passing of the days. And, perhaps most significantly, no environmental destruction anywhere near the scale we've been witnessing for the past few hundred years. Just the land, the water, and the sky.

Our oldest ancestors lived in this world.

They shared an intimate connection with the earth and the elements in a way we couldn't imagine today. They received information directly from the natural world and its turning seasons. Through the bounty of the Earth and the workings of the elements of rain, sun, air, and fire, they participated in the natural cycle of life.

They harvested the Earth's wild abundance to make food and medicine, and they worked with the Earth intentionally to create growth through crops and livestock. In the millennia before what we've come to call the Information Age, they learned what they needed to know about the world and its wonders from what their surroundings taught them. To survive their primitive circumstances, they had to pay attention.

And pay attention they did! Surviving ruins of ancient monuments around the world demonstrate the sophisticated knowledge our ancestors gained from studying the sky. The Mayans incorporated observations of the cycles of the Moon and Venus into their calendar systems. A pre-Celtic farming community in Ireland created an ancient temple mound with a passage that is illuminated only by the Winter Solstice Sun.

These accomplishments didn't arise solely out of close study, but were created in the context of a spiritual relationship with the cosmos. Mayan myths credit the god Itzamná with giving them the knowledge of the calendar system—and although we don't know the exact details, the ancient, unknown peoples of Ireland clearly involved a deity of some kind in their works.

The pre-written history of Wicca draws on the primal energy of this relationship to the natural world. Whatever the particular tradition or form the practice of Wicca follows, this connection with the forces all around us is the basis.

Wiccans know that although the world has been dramatically transformed by the impact of human presence, the basics remain the same, as our most essential requirements for survival have not changed. In this spirit, Wicca adopts and adapts its traditions both from what is known about our ancestors' ways of life, and from what is imagined, collectively and individually. The continuity may be considered symbolic rather than literal, but in grounding the Wiccan worldview in the realities of nature, Wiccans and Witches create a life of attunement with what some call "All That Is."

So Wiccans Worship Nature?

Wicca embraces the existence of two main deities, who are generically called the Goddess and the God, but who may go by a myriad of other names. They are, according to Wiccans, the original Deities, the female and male forces of nature that make all life possible. In one sense, Wicca can be called a duotheistic religion, though it's more complex than that, as many other deities from many ancient cultures are also likely to enter the picture (we'll cover this shortly!).

Some Wiccans believe that the Goddess and God are the *supreme* deities and all other gods and goddesses are lesser forms of deity. Others hold the perspective that the Goddess is comprised of all goddesses, and that each goddess is a particular aspect of the female power source, collectively called the Goddess. Likewise, all gods are individual aspects of the God.

Some traditions alternatively call these two deities "the Lord and the Lady," though in terms of its historical connotations, this pair of words implies a somewhat hierarchical, rather than equal, relationship—Wiccans believe the God and the Goddess are completely equal, although you may personally feel more affinity to one over the other.

For example, some eclectic Wiccans may, in their spiritual orientation to the divine, favor the male aspect of deity over the female to a degree, while others, especially followers of Dianic Wicca, pay far more attention to the female. Whatever the case, in its most basic form the relationship is between equals, as both female and male energies make up life on earth. In the natural world, one cannot exist without the other.

Representations of the Goddess and the God in Wicca tend to symbolize the principle functions of life creation that are the dominion of the female and male forces. The God is associated with the Sun, and also very often referred to and depicted as the Horned God. The Goddess, associated with the Moon, is actually comprised of three aspects—the Maiden, the Mother, and the Crone—which are represented by the cycles of the Moon. She is often called simply The Triple Goddess.

THE HORNED GOD / THE SUN GOD

Across many old European pagan cultures, a common deity appears, known as the Horned God, who is the ruler of wild animals and the hunting activities of humans. As a symbol of his connection with the animals of the forests and plains, he is often depicted with horns on his head, like those of the stag. He is also associated with the Sun and its role in the growing and harvesting of the food provided by the Earth. Older cultures called the God and Goddess the Sky Father and Earth Mother, identifying each deity's place in the continuation of the life cycle.

As the ruler of the Sun, the God is also associated with fire and light, and it is his journey around the Earth that shapes the cycle of Wiccan rituals in the year, beginning with Winter, then following the natural course of Spring, Summer, and Autumn, and back to Winter for the beginning of a new year. The Sun is said to be the source of all life, and so the God is also associated with sex, the procreative act that generates new life, and is often represented in phallic symbols such as the previously mentioned horns, as well as spears, swords, wands, and arrows.

Some of the deities from the world's pantheon who represent the God are the Greek gods Pan, Adonis, and Dionysus, the Egyptian Osiris, and the Celtic Cernnunos and Lugh.

THE GODDESS / THE TRIPLE GODDESS

If the God, as the Sky Father, is the source of all life, the Goddess, as the Earth Mother, is the source that sustains life and allows it to flourish.

As a nurturing and tending essence, she is also associated with domesticated animals. Her realm of influence includes the Earth and its oceans, as well as the Moon that creates the tides. Other names for her include the Great Mother and the Divine Source. Symbols associated with the Goddess reflect the receptive aspect of sex such as the cup and cauldron, as well as her gift of abundance, such as certain flowers and fruits. In various Wiccan cosmologies, she may be represented by the Greek Diana, the Egyptian Isis, and the Celtic Brigid, among others.

As the female force that sustains life, the Goddess in modern Wicca is represented by three aspects which mirror both the life cycle of women and the phases of the Moon. Some written and pictorial representations from ancient societies show her as having three faces, one representing each aspect. In some traditions, she is called the Triple Moon Goddess, recognizing the power source that is the Moon. In others, the balance of association with Earth as well as the Moon is reflected in the less specific name Triple Goddess. Each aspect of the

Goddess has its role in the life cycle of the Earth and its inhabitants.

The Maiden

The Maiden aspect aligns with the crescent phase of the Moon. She is the growth phase of life, reflected in the waxing of the Moon as it moves toward fullness. She's associated with the season of Spring and with youth, innocence, and independence. Goddesses representing the Maiden include the Greek goddesses Persephone and Artemis, the Celtic Rhiannon, the Hindu Parvati, and the Nordic Freya.

The Mother

When the Moon waxes to full, the Goddess becomes the Mother, the source of the Earth's abundance. She's associated with Summer, and the lush time of year when plant and animal life matures into fullness. This is considered by many Witches to be the most powerful aspect of the Goddess. The Mother is represented by the Greek Demeter and Selene, the Roman Ceres, and the Celtic Badb and Danu, among others.

The Crone

The waning of the Moon belongs to the Crone, who is a symbol of death as part of the life cycle, and of the wisdom gained from a full and productive life. She is associated with the time of Autumn and Winter, the winding down and ending of the growing season. She completes the cycle of the Moon and the cycle of death and rebirth in all living things. The cycle begins again at the New Moon when the Maiden returns. Goddesses associated with death and the underworld often represent her, such as the Greek Hecate, the Russian Baba Yaga, and the Celtic Morrigan and Cailleach Bear.

EVERYONE ELSE

As was noted above, Wicca is more a polytheistic religion than a duotheistic one, since many different gods and goddesses may represent the Goddess and God. Furthermore, other deities can be part of Wiccan ritual in their own right, in addition to the main deities.

Many Wiccans cultivate individual, personal relationships with one or more deities from a range of ancient cultures across the globe, though most commonly from ancient Greco-Roman, Egyptian, and Celtic peoples. In this sense, Wicca is also a pantheistic religion, in that it is inclusive rather than exclusive when it comes to deities, and doesn't view the material world as inherently separate from deity.

The *encouragement* to find one's own personal relationships or affinities with deities of one's choice is another aspect of Wicca that sets it apart from most other religions.

People entering the Craft will study the myths and other known information and look for feelings of affinity with one or more deities in particular. They will also meditate on the possibilities and see which tend to "speak" to them on an intuitive level. Choices of alignments might be rooted in an ethnic or regional preference (for example, many Witches of Celtic descent tend to favor the Celtic pantheon), but are definitely not limited to these parameters, as the many aspects of deity are relevant to Witches for all kinds of reasons. Wiccans don't necessarily stay aligned with the same deities for their entire lives—new relationships may arise at different points in a person's life in response to new situations or circumstances.

In traditional Wicca, covens often center their worship and affiliations on one god and goddess as aspects of the deities. Members are free to have their own personal alignments with other deities of their choosing, but in formal ritual will work with the deities the coven is devoted to.

Understanding the Wiccan relationship with the deities begins with a look at how their holidays and rituals observe and celebrate the natural cycle of life. Ritual is where the most focused interaction with the Goddess and God takes place. Wiccans and other Witches pay homage to their chosen forms of deity and may work magical spells to bring manifestations of needs and wishes, both personal and collective.

THE WHEEL OF THE YEAR

Wicca is called an "earth" religion in part because its worship traditions are anchored to the natural cycles seen here on Earth, for example the turning of the seasons.

In an age when we are removed from nature by technological advances and endless distractions, marking the Wheel of the Year becomes a way to reconnect with the Divine essence of life and the Earth's role in our existence. Some Witches refer to their participation in the Wiccan holidays, known as Sabbats, as "Turning the Wheel," to emphasize our co-creative relationship with nature.

The Wiccan year is not the same as the standard Gregorian calendar, which begins on January 1st. Instead, it follows the four seasons, marking the progress in the Earth's path around the Sun (which appears, of course, to be the Sun's journey around the Earth) and the corresponding changes to life on Earth. Wicca has eight major holidays, or Sabbats, four of which are "solar holidays": the Winter and Summer Solstices, and the Spring and Autumn Equinoxes. The other four Sabbats, or the "Earth festivals," occur near the "cross-quarter days" between the solar holidays, and are based on older pagan folk festivals which are thought to have been linked to the life cycles of animals and agriculture.

Note: The dates for the solar Sabbats are given as a range to account for differences in the Sun's position in the sky relative to where one lives. The seasonal names for the Solstices and Equinoxes, as well as the seasonal associations with each Sabbat, are also different in the Southern Hemisphere.

The existence of eight Sabbats, rather than four, acknowledges that the contemporary delineations we mark between "the four seasons" are somewhat artificial. For example, Spring does not suddenly turn into Summer on June 21st—it has been moving in that direction for some time before the modern calendar recognizes it as "Summer."

In fact, an old name for the Summer Solstice is actually "Midsummer," recognizing that Summer has been well underway by the time the Sun reaches its zenith in the sky. The cross-quarter Sabbats mark the "seasons in-between seasons" and guide the ongoing transitions along the Wheel of the Year. The Sabbats are considered "days of power" and are marked by Wiccans, Witches, and other Pagans of many traditions.

THE SABBATS

Winter Solstice (Yule): December 20-23

Considered in most Wiccan traditions to be the beginning of the year, the Winter Solstice is a celebration of the rebirth of the God. It is the shortest day of the year, offering a welcome reminder that even though the cold season is still just getting underway, it doesn't last forever, as the days will begin to lengthen again after this point. Some consider the first Full Moon after the Solstice to be the most powerful of the year. This is a festive holiday celebrating light, as well as preparation for a time of quiet, inner focus as the Earth rests from her labor.

Among many Wiccans the holiday is more commonly called "Yule," a name derived from midwinter festivals celebrated by Germanic tribes. "Yule" is still referenced in modern Christmas carols, and many of the traditions surrounding the Christian holiday, such as wreaths, Christmas trees, and caroling have their roots in these older traditions. It was common for the Christian churches to "adopt" pagan holidays, repurposing them for celebrating saints or important events, as a way of drawing people away from the Old Religion.

Imbolc: February 2

Imbolc marks the first stirrings of Spring, as the long months of Winter are nearly past. The Goddess is beginning her recovery after the birth of the God, and the lengthening days signal the strengthening of the God's power. Seeds begin to germinate, daffodils appear, and hibernating animals start to emerge from their slumber. It is a time for ritual cleansing after a long period of inactivity. Covens may perform initiation rites at this time of new beginnings.

The name "Imbolc" is derived from an Old Irish word used to describe the pregnancy of ewes and has been sometimes translated as meaning "ewe's milk," in reference to the birthing of the first lambs of the season. It is also called "Candlemas," and sometimes "Brigid's Day" in Irish traditions. Associated with beginnings of growth, it's considered a festival of the Maiden.

Spring Equinox (Ostara): March 20-23

At the Spring Equinox, light and dark are finally equal again, and growth accelerates as both the light from the still-young God of the Sun and the fertility of the Earth grow more powerful. Gardening begins in earnest and trees send out blossoms to participate with the pollinating bees. The equal length of day and night brings about a time for balancing and bringing opposing forces into harmony.

The name "Ostara" comes from the Saxon Eostre, the Goddess of Spring and renewal. This is where the name Easter comes from, as this is another holiday that was "merged" with the Christian tradition.

Beltane: May 1

As Spring begins to move into Summer, the Goddess begins making her transition into the Mother aspect, and the God matures into his full potency. Beltane is a fire festival, and a celebration of love, sex, and reproduction. It's at this time that the Goddess couples with the God to ensure his rebirth after his death at the end of the life cycle. Fertility is at its height and the Earth prepares to flourish with new life.

The name "Beltane" comes from an ancient festival celebrated throughout the Celtic Isles that marked the beginning of Summer, and is derived from an old Celtic word meaning "bright fire." The ancient Irish would light giant fires to purify and protect their cattle, and jumping over fires was considered a way to increase fertility and luck in the coming season.

Summer Solstice / Midsummer: June 20-23

Long considered one of the most magical times of the year, the Summer Solstice sees the God and the Goddess at the peak of their powers. The Sun is at its highest point and the days are at their longest. This is a celebration of the abundance of sunlight and warmth, and the physical manifestation of abundance as the year heads toward the first of the harvests. It's a time of ease and of brief rest after the work of planting and before the work of harvesting begins.

Some traditions call this Sabbat "Litha," a name traced back to an old Anglo-Saxon word for this time of year.

Lammas: August 1

Lammas marks the beginning of the harvest season. The first crops are brought in from the fields, the trees and plants begin dropping their fruits and seeds, and the days are growing shorter as the God's power begins to wane. This is a time for giving thanks for the abundance of the growing season as it begins to wind down.

The word Lammas stems from an old Anglo-Saxon word pairing meaning "loaf mass," and it was customary to bless fresh loaves of bread as a way of celebrating the harvest. Lammas is alternately known as "Lughnasa," after the traditional festivals in Ireland and Scotland held at this time to honor the Celtic god Lugh, who was associated with the Sun.

Autumn Equinox (Mabon): September 20-23

The harvest season is still in focus at the Autumn Equinox. The animals born during the year have matured, and the trees are beginning to lose their leaves. Preparations are made for the coming winter. The God is making his exit from the physical plane and heading toward his mythical death at Samhain, and his ultimate rebirth at Yule. Once again, the days and nights are of equal length, symbolizing the temporary nature of all life—no season lasts forever, and neither dark nor light ever overpowers the other for long. As with the Spring Equinox on the opposite side of the Wheel, balance is a theme at this time.

The Autumn Equinox is considered in some traditions to be "the Second Harvest," with Lammas as the first and Samhain as the last of three harvests. A more recent name for the holiday is "Mabon," after a Welsh mythological figure whose origins are connected to a divine "mother and son" pair, echoing the dual nature of the relationship between the Goddess and the God.

Samhain: October 31

Considered by many Wiccans to be the most important of the Sabbats, Samhain is the time when the part death plays in the cycle of life is acknowledged and honored. The word "Samhain" comes from old Irish and is thought by many to mean "Summer's end," though others trace it to a root word meaning "assembly," which may refer to the communal gathering of a pagan festival, especially during the harvest season. As the Sun aspect, the God retreats into the shadows as night begins to dominate the day. As the God of the Hunt, he is a reminder of the sacrifice of life that keeps us alive through the long winter months. The harvest is complete and the sacred nature of food is respected. Among some traditions this is viewed as the "Third Harvest."

Wiccan and other pagan traditions view Samhain as a point in the Wheel when the "veil" between the spiritual and material worlds is at its thinnest, and the days around Samhain are considered especially effective for divination activities of all kinds. Ancestors are honored and communicated with at this time. Many of the Halloween traditions still celebrated in contemporary cultures today can be traced back through the centuries to this festival. Pagans of the old times left food offerings for their ancestors, which became the modern custom of trick-or-treating. Jack-o-lanterns evolved from the practice of leaving candle-lit hollowed-out root vegetables to guide spirits visiting on Earth.

Some Wiccans in the Celtic traditions consider Samhain, as opposed to Yule, to be the beginning of the year, as the death and rebirth aspects of creation are seen to be inherently joined together—death opens the space for new life to take root. Honoring the ancient Celtic view of the year having a "light half" and a "dark half," their Wheel of the Year begins anew on this day, the first day of the dark half of the year.

THE ESBATS

In addition to the Sabbats, the Wiccan year contains 12 (sometimes 13) Full Moon celebrations, known as the Esbats. While the Sabbats tend to focus celebration on the God and his association with the Sun, the Esbats honor the Goddess in her association with the Moon. Covens traditionally meet on the Esbats to celebrate a particular aspect of the Goddess, such as Aphrodite, in a celebration of abundance, or Persephone, in a ritual for renewal. They work with the Goddess to bring about healing and assistance for their members and communities, and often work for the good of the wider world as well.

The Full Moon is also seen within the context of the Wheel of the Year, with names and seasonal attributions for each. For Wiccans working with particular aspects of the Goddess, the specific goddess called upon during an Esbat will often correspond with the time of year. For example, Aphrodite is an appropriate goddess to celebrate abundance under a Summer Moon, whereas Persephone, with her underworld associations, is more appropriate to work with under a late Autumn or early Winter Moon.

The names for each Moon may vary from tradition to tradition, but are generally related to the time of year and the corresponding level of abundance and activity of life on Earth, as well as the Sun's point in its journey around the Earth. In the Northern Hemisphere, the most typical names for the Full Moons in Wiccan rituals are as follows:

Month	Moon Name
January	Cold Moon (also Hunger)
February	Quickening Moon (also Snow)
March	Storm Moon (also Sap)
April	Wind Moon (also Pink)
May	Flower Moon (also Milk)
June	Sun Moon (also Strong Sun and Rose)
July	Blessing Moon (also Thunder)
August	Corn Moon (also Grain)
September	Harvest Moon
October	Blood Moon
November	Mourning Moon (also Frost)
December	Long Nights Moon

Many Witches consider astrological influences in addition to seasonal influences and will work according to the particular sign the Moon is in while full. They will refer to the Moon accordingly, such as the "Gemini Moon" or the "Aquarius Moon."

When more than one Full Moon occurs in a given calendar month, it's called a Blue Moon. Occurring roughly once every two and a half years, this is considered a particularly powerful time in many Wiccan traditions, and special attention is paid to working with the rare energy of a Blue Moon.

THE ELEMENTS

One way of connecting with the energies of the natural world, and by extension, the entire Universe, is in relationship with the Four Elements.

The recognition of elemental states of matter has been around since the ancient Greeks, and versions of the concept appear in a number of cultures with ancient lineages. In Wicca and other pagan belief systems, the Elements are seen as fundamental aspects of divine energy, each containing qualities that manifest in our personalities and our way of being in the world. They are an important component of Wiccan ritual, where each element is represented in the tangible forms of colors, tools, natural objects, instruments and herbs, and the intangible forms of the four cardinal directions, the four seasons, particular deities, and, often, astrological signs.

Working with the Elements can help increase certain desired energies and experiences such as love and abundance, and can help balance unwanted experiences rooted in the negative qualities inherent in personalities.

Let's take a look at the four elements, in turn.

Earth

The Earth is the center of our human universe, providing us the foundation of life and keeping us literally grounded through its gravitational pull. It's the source of all sustaining plant and animal life that provide nourishment and healing. It can cause physical death and destruction through earthquakes, mudslides and avalanches.

The Earth is physically represented by many of its topographical features, such as rocks, soil, caves, fields, forests, and gardens. The Element of Earth is associated with strength, abundance, and prosperity, and is represented by the colors green, yellow, brown, and black. Earth energy is feminine and receptive. Positive qualities associated with Earth are stability, responsibility, respect, and endurance, while negative qualities include stubbornness and rigidity. The Earth's cardinal direction is North, and its season is Winter.

Air

Air is the invisible Element. Its presence is only seen in the effects it has on other matter—leaves fluttering in the breeze, the movement of the clouds. Although it can't be seen itself, it can be felt all around us, which may be why it's associated with the mind, the intellect, communication and divination.

It's also associated with sky, wind, mountaintops and birds, and is represented in yellow, white, and silver, among other colors. Air is essential for life as it carries oxygen, and it contributes to abundance by carrying and spreading seeds to new places where they can sprout. It also participates in the destructive force of life with storms and frigid wind. It is a masculine, projective energy. Positive personal qualities associated with Air energy include intelligence, inspiration, and optimism. Negative qualities include gossip and forgetfulness. Air's cardinal direction is East, and its season is Spring.

Fire

The awesome, destructive potential of Fire is probably most striking in the seasonal wildfires that burn millions of acres of forest around the world, and can actually jump over rivers and roads to resume their spread on the other side. Lightning can also be deadly, as can extreme heat. Of course, Fire is also life-sustaining, used for cooking and lighting for over 100,000 years.

The Element of Fire is associated with the Sun, sunlight, stars, deserts, and volcanoes. It is represented with red, gold, crimson, orange, and white, and is a masculine, projective energy. Fire is the Element of transformation illumination, health, and strength. Its positive qualities promote love, passion, enthusiasm, courage, and leadership. Negative qualities include hate, jealousy, fear, anger, and conflict. Its season is Summer, and South is its cardinal direction.

Water

Water is essential for life on Earth and is present in all life. It established forms in the Earth such as lakes and rivers by following the path of least resistance, and can wear away solid rock over time. It is associated with all of its visible physical manifestations, such as streams, springs, oceans, the rain, and the Moon, which exerts its own gravitational pull on Water's most massive forms. Its destructive forces manifest in severe rainstorms, floods, whirlpools and riptides.

Its Elemental energy is associated with emotions, healing, dreams, psychic clairvoyance and the subconscious. Water is receptive, feminine, and represented by blue, green, indigo and black. Its positive qualities include compassion, forgiveness, and intuition. Negative qualities are laziness, indifference, insecurity, and lack of control over emotions. Autumn is Water's season, and its cardinal direction is West.

The Fifth Element: Spirit

Many Wiccan traditions recognize a Fifth Element which is referred to as "Aether," or, more commonly, "Spirit."

This is the Element present in all things, immaterial but essential for connection and balance between all other

Elements. It has been described as the binding force through which manifestation is made possible, as well as the divine intelligence of the "All" that spiritualists of many traditions seek connection with. The Fifth Element is also known as "Akasha," from the Sanskrit word for "aether," which is found in Buddhism, Hinduism, and other religions, and is translated by some as "inner space" or "open space."

The Fifth Element is represented by the color white. Unlike the other Elements, it has no gender, energy type, or cardinal direction. It has no season, but is rather associated with the entire Wheel of the Year.

OTHER BELIEFS

Borrowing as it does from many older spiritual traditions, Wicca is inherently a "patch-worked" system of beliefs. In addition to relationship with deity and the participation in the natural cycles of life, other beliefs and practices contribute to the Wiccan religion.

These beliefs are as personal and idiosyncratic as the choice of deities one resonates with, and include reincarnation, animism, the existence of unseen dimensions, sometimes called "the Otherworld," and the existence of fairies and/or other unseen spirits.

REINCARNATION

A major tenet among Wiccans, the idea that we live many times over in different times and places on Earth is found in several religions, including Jainism, Hinduism, and Buddhism, as well as in other ancient and modern cultures.

Wicca has adopted this belief in many ways, which differ from coven to coven and individual to individual. While some Witches believe that we can and sometimes do choose to reincarnate in non-human forms—i.e. as animals or plants—many others believe that we only come back as humans.

Either way, reincarnation is seen as a logical extension of the life/death/life cycle observed in nature and celebrated throughout the Wheel of the Year. It is also used as a lens through which to look at life struggles and lessons, as the belief that we've chosen our life circumstances before being born into our new bodies is common.

While it's never possible to scientifically verify the existence of past lives, many Wiccans and other spiritual seekers feel to be aware of at least some details of a past before this life, while others may have a sense of having "been here" before. This feeling may occur in or near a particular place where a past life was lived, or manifest in an affinity for a particular time period in history or a country or continent that has never been visited in this lifetime. A common "past life history" among Witches involves at least one prior life as a Witch, often one that ended in some form of persecution. Many of these Witches feel they have chosen to come back at a time when their form of religion is accepted—at least enough not to put them in real danger.

Wiccans and spiritual healers of many traditions today employ meditation, past-life regression, and dream analysis techniques to help people recall their past lives as a way of understanding their current problems. It is thought that whatever spiritual lessons were not learned in the past can be actively worked on in this life, which sets up the soul to learn new lessons, both in this and future lives.

THE AFTERLIFE

Wiccans generally believe in an afterlife of some form or another. However, this is not an "absolute" place where we remain for eternity—for example the Christian Heaven and Hell—but rather the place where our souls spend time between incarnations.

Names and descriptions for this realm vary widely and may be based on older belief traditions or be more idiosyncratic, with each individual's experience and perception informing her or his notion of what's beyond that which we can physically perceive as this life. The spiritual realm is known as the Otherworld, the Afterworld, Summerland, and the Shining Land, among other names. Some describe it as a naturally abundant and beautiful place, while others see it more as an entity that doesn't resemble any physical reality on Earth.

It is nevertheless interconnected with all things in the Universe and many who practice divination believe it to be the source of the answers to their questions. It is thought by some Wiccans that the afterlife is a place to make choices about our next incarnations based on what we've learned, or haven't yet learned, so far in our soul's journey.

ANIMISM

In its most basic form, animism is the belief that everything in the material world has a "soul" or a "spirit." This applies to all non-human animals as well as the geographical and ecological phenomena of rocks, trees, and anything else found on Earth. Many indigenous cultures operate from an animistic perspective, including several Native American belief systems and the traditional Japanese Shinto religion.

Animism provides a way of seeing into the divine relationship between humans and the natural world, as particular stones, trees, and streams may be imbued with a special sense of energy and held as sacred sites of worship. The Celtic belief in fairies (also spelled "faeries") can be seen as a form of animism, as they are themselves generally invisible but thought to live in hills, mounds, woodlands, and other natural phenomena.

For some, animism also powers the workings of magic, as objects used in ritual may be thought to possess their own spirit energies, which are joined with those of the Witch to effect the positive change being sought.

OTHER OCCULT SYSTEMS

The ancient traditions of astrology provide a way to view events on Earth as being influenced by the energies and locations of celestial bodies. Astrological systems vary from culture to culture, but Wicca tends to incorporate Western astrology with its focus on the Sun, the Moon, the planets of our Solar System, and the other stars of the Milky Way Galaxy.

The signs of the Zodiac wheel, which measures the Sun's path across the celestial sphere according to how it looks from Earth, are named for constellations and assigned "ruling" planets that influence behavior and phenomena in particular ways. The horoscopes that most people are familiar with today represent only a fraction of the information contained in astrology, as they tend to focus solely on a person's Sun sign. The full picture of a person's personality makeup and potential life paths is much more complex.

Many Wiccans know at least the basics of their astrological birth charts—their Sun sign, Moon sign and Rising sign—as well as the general "personality type" of each sign in the Zodiac wheel. The current position of both the Sun and Moon at any given time is often taken into consideration when working magic for a particular purpose. The Moon's current sign is especially important for Esbats, with different signs being more or less favorable for specific intentions. And some Witches mark the four Earth Sabbats (Imbolc, Beltane, Lammas, and Samhain) by the zodiacal midpoint between the nearest solar holidays, or "cross quarter" days, rather than on the modern calendar dates, so that Beltane, for example, is celebrated on February 4th instead of February 2nd.

Numerology is an occult system of assigning spiritual and/or magical qualities to the numbers 0-9 (and, in some traditions, 11 and 22). Each number has its own energy and characteristics that manifest as personality traits and life experiences.

For example, people who are assigned the number 6 based on the date of their birth or the letters in their names are said to be very family oriented, and their lives will reflect this. Numerological significances can be incorporated into Wiccan practice in ritual, magic, and divination methods. The number 3 is particularly significant to Wiccans, as seen in the many versions of the Triple Goddess. Some Wiccans choose a sacred "Wiccan name" for themselves based on numerological systems.

Finally, different methods and traditions of divination are often part of Wiccan practice. Witches use Tarot cards, pendulums, runes, the Celtic Ogham, and objects for "scrying" such as crystal balls, mirrors, and the surface of still water to communicate with unseen energies and discover the hidden forces at work in their unfolding lives.

Witches might consult their preferred divination tools for insight into how best to set their intentions for a coming ritual. Divination may also be part of ritual or occur immediately after, but can be practiced at any time. Astrology and numerology are often intertwined with certain divination practices, especially in Tarot and other forms of divination cards.

THE NEXT STEP

Now that we've taken a brief look at the origins and the basic belief systems of modern Wicca, let's take a closer look at how these belief systems are enacted through religious ritual, magical spellwork, and general daily life.

INTRODUCTION TO WITCHCRAFT

WHAT IS WITCHCRAFT?

As noted previously, those who identify as Wiccans and those who identify as Witches have differences of opinion regarding the term "Witchcraft." While not all Witchcraft is considered to be specifically "Wiccan," the terms "Wicca" and "Witchcraft" are often used interchangeably.

Some Wiccans argue for a distinction between what they consider to be spirituality-based worship ("Wicca") and more "secular" magical practice ("Witchcraft"), but more often the two are intertwined enough that the distinction isn't particularly useful.

With all due respect to Wiccans who recognize a difference, the term "Witchcraft" will be used in this guide to describe the general activities found in rituals practiced by Wiccans and non-Wiccan Witches alike. Because some Wiccans do not practice magic and do not consider themselves Witches, the term "Witch" in this section of the guide is meant to refer those who both adopt Wiccan practices in some form or another *and* practice magic as part of their religion.

Still with me? Great, let's take a look at Witchcraft and magic in more detail.

Witchcraft is the set of beliefs and practices employed by Witches in ritual and spellwork. Often, magical work is incorporated into the Sabbat and Esbat celebrations observed by covens and solitary Witches, though spellwork may be employed on its own on other occasions. In fact, many Witches consider themselves to be constantly "practicing" their Craft in their daily lives through the use of meditation, magically charged meals and beverages, color choices in clothing and jewelry, nightly candle rituals, and other seemingly "small" enactments of magic. The more one is in tune with the rhythms and energies of the natural world, the more "magical" one's life will seem and feel, and this relationship with the cycles of life is deepened throughout one's life through study and practice.

"Magic" is a word used for the phenomena that occur when people consciously participate in the co-creative forces of the Universe, by using the subtle energies of nature to cause desired change in their reality.

People may use magic, or "the Craft" as it is often called, for many purposes. This often includes spells, charms, and other workings for what could be called "personal gain," such as a new job or improvements in a love relationship. However, the Craft is also used to work for benefits to one's family, community, or even to people across the globe. For example, a coven may use an Esbat ritual as an opportunity to send beneficial healing light to victims of a natural disaster. What the Craft is definitely *not* used for is anything that would cause harm to another person or other living being, even unintentionally. Our wishes can often be manipulative when it comes to how they affect other people, even when we don't realize it. Therefore, ritual and spellwork often include safeguards against accidental misuse of magical energy, such as the phrases "for the good of all" and "harm to none"—taken from the Wiccan rede. Keeping this idea in the forefront of one's mind is important, particularly in light of another basic tenet of Witchcraft: the Threefold Law.

Also known as "The Rule of Three" and "The Law of Return," this principle states that whatever Witches send out into the Universe as intent, whether positive or negative, will come back to them three times as great. While some Witches don't subscribe to this particular belief, it is often invoked as a reminder that magical power should be used only for good, and never in the spirit of harm or manipulation.

MAGIC AND SCIENCE

Many contemporary writers on Witchcraft have pointed out the relevance of new discoveries in the physical sciences that seem to identify what Witches have always known to exist: a symbiotic relationship between mind and matter.

This relationship can be viewed from many angles and is probably not entirely understood by anyone, but its existence is clear to practitioners of magic as well as other mind/thought-based disciplines that bring about positive change in one's life.

The traditional worldview of most of Western society for the past few millennia has held that reality is chaotic and inflexible, created by forces outside of human control. It has also held that the mind is not a physical entity, and is separate from what we think of as "matter." (The phrase "mind over matter" illustrates the fundamental opposition perceived to exist between the two.) What Witches understand, and what science has begun to uncover, is that reality is flexible, and *is* co-created by and with everything in it, including the mind. Mind is not separate from matter, but *is* matter in its most basic form.

The power of thought has been illuminated in many books and videos about the "Law of Attraction," a "New Age" topic that has recently found popularity among mainstream audiences, celebrities, and even business professionals. The Law states that thoughts attract experiences that reinforce them, so that dwelling on negative circumstances can keep them in place, while focusing on positive experiences creates improved circumstances. Changing one's thoughts is harder than it might seem, of course, which is possibly why so much information and advice regarding the Law of Attraction is currently available.

The Hermetic Principle

Witchcraft can be said to employ the Law of Attraction in a sense, though magic can be much more complex than simply focusing one's thoughts on a desired outcome. It might be more accurate to say that Witches employ rituals, tools, words, and gifts from the natural world to enhance and expand their work with the Hermetic Principles, which are where the Law of Attraction comes from.

The Hermetic Principles date back to late antiquity and have informed Western religious, philosophical, esoteric and scientific thought. They have interesting parallels in modern physics, including quantum mechanics and string theory, and describe the way reality operates on a subatomic level, where all material things are composed of energy and radiate energy. Many Witches have been watching excitedly as the scientific understanding of the makeup of the Universe unfolds to confirm what ancient observers knew.

There are seven Hermetic Principles (also known as "Hermetic Laws"), which are often referred to in discussions of magic. One of the most emphasized is the Law of Correspondence, which states that what is true on the macrocosm is also true on the microcosm. This means that every particle of matter contains all others—and that linear time on the physical plane represents only one dimension in the ultimately spaceless and timeless overall Universe. Another way of stating the principle is "as above, so below; as below, so above." The higher planes of existence influence the lower planes of existence, and vice versa. As microcosms of the Universe, we are able to glean information from the distant past, view images of the future through divination, and change our reality.

A recent and widely-reported study found that the laws governing the growth of the Universe share significant similarities to the growth of both the human brain and the Internet. This is an interesting illustration of the Law of Correspondence, and also provides a window into the Law of Mentalism, another important principle of Witchcraft.

Just as every particle of matter contains all others, matter and energy all contain information at their most basic level. The Universe, ultimately, is mental at its highest level, which is the underlying creative force of all things. We know that all the inventions, developments, and adaptations in our human history began as ideas. Witches also know that thoughts can influence the Universal mind, and this is part of why focused intention in ritual is important.

The Law of Vibration holds that everything is in constant motion, and that nothing is at rest. This applies even to seemingly sturdy physical objects such as chairs and tables—they have vibrations than we simply can't perceive with the human mind. Matter is composed of energy, which is essentially a force moving at a certain vibration. The parallel with animism is worth noting here, as animists believe that everything is alive. If a characteristic of being "alive" is to be in motion, then the animists have been correct all along.

The nature of colors as light moving at different rates of vibration is particularly useful in Witchcraft, as each color's frequency has particular characteristics suitable for specific purposes. We often associate love with the colors red and pink, for example, and it turns out that these colors resonate with energies in the body that promote loving feelings. Therefore, these colors, when used in spellwork to bring love into one's life, both communicate that information to the Universe and connect it to the Witch's energy field. Of course, like all things, colors can have their down sides. The intense vibration of red can also overstimulate and trigger unpleasant feelings. Color therapies using the Chakra system and meditation techniques often seek to balance out-of-whack vibrations in the body, and colors can be used magically in much the same way.

Understanding systems like the Hermetic Principles and the Law of Attraction can be helpful in increasing one's success in magic, but a thorough grounding in them is not entirely necessary. And it's helpful to remember that no matter how powerful the intentions for magic may be, results may be limited by the endless unknown realities of the physical and higher planes—sometimes we're just not meant to get exactly what we want at a particular time. It may be that someone else would be harmed in some way, or that something else is already around the corner that will take care of our needs in a different way.

In fact, Witches can learn a lot about the nature of the Universe by observing which of their magical workings succeed, and which do not. The study of the Craft is considered by most to be a lifelong pursuit, with ongoing learning and refining of practices. The wisdom of ongoing study makes even more sense when considering the parallels between the growth of the Universe and the growth of the human brain. As more learning occurs, more magical techniques are invented and developed, and there's all the more to catch up on.

RITUAL AND SPELLWORK

It might be said that Wicca, as a religion, recognizes the laws of the Universe symbolically through the Goddess and God, the Wheel of the Year, and reverence for all living things.

Rituals performed in celebration of these aspects of the Universe may or may not involve magical work, as some Wiccans prefer to focus on what they view as the "spiritual" side of life. Witches, on the other hand, tend to blend ritual with magic, and may actually focus solely on working to transform reality for the benefit of themselves and others. This doesn't necessarily mean they don't consider themselves spiritual. Indeed, if all matter contains all matter, then there really is no separation between spiritual concerns and the concerns of everyday life.

Whether or not magic is being worked in a given ritual, Wiccans and other Witches tend to incorporate a few common structures in their formal activities, including casting a sacred or magical circle, invoking deities and/or particular powers using special words and phrases, and closing the circle at the end of the ritual. Movement, dance, chanting or singing may also be part of the activities.

These formal steps communicate to the higher realms of the Universe the thoughts and intentions of the practitioner(s) in a focused and effective manner, concentrating the energies of intention clearly and definitively. Energy, as physical matter, is raised in ritual and directed toward specific purposes, whether for gratitude and celebration, manifesting solutions to problems, or both.

Casting the Circle

As a symbol, the circle represents the Moon, the Earth, and the abundance of the Goddess. For this reason, a circle is able to safely contain the physical quantity of energy raised by the Witch or Witches performing the ritual, and see its transformation through to the higher realms. The circle is an infinitely portable tool, as it can be drawn anywhere, either physically or psychically, subtly or elaborately, depending on the circumstances.

The circle is as big or small as appropriate, but has to have enough room for the altar, everything being used in the ritual, and everyone participating—I'll be introducing to you the altar and ritual tools in the next section. It is usually marked on the floor of the space being used for ritual, often with sea salt first, followed by candles, or other magical items charged with energy for the purpose of ritual, such as crystals and semiprecious gemstones, or even herbs.

Once energy is raised inside the circle, the circle must remain closed until the end of the ritual. This keeps the energy from mingling with inappropriate or distracting energy from the rest of the physical plane, which strengthens the magic and protects practitioners from unwanted energetic interference.

No one can step outside of the circle while it is active without first performing an energetic manipulation, such as a "circle-cutting" spell, which creates an energetic "doorway" that is safe to exit and reenter. Once the circle is reentered, the door is closed and the circle reconnected.

Calling the Quarters

Also referred to as "drawing the quarters" this is a way of acknowledging the four cardinal directions and their Elemental associations, as well as the chosen deities of the coven or solitary Witch.

In a coven, either the High Priestess, the High Priest, or another coven member will walk around the circle, stopping in each cardinal direction to invoke the presence of its associated Element and, if applicable, god or goddess. (It should be remembered here that not all coven structures involve hierarchy—some covens simply have each member take turns performing this and any other necessary roles in ritual.) Specific words are usually spoken to invoke the specific powers and blessings of the element and/or deity being called. Once this is complete, the space is ready for the heart of the ritual.

Types of Ritual

The heart of the ritual may be a Sabbat or Esbat celebration, or it may celebrate a life event such as an initiation into a coven, a self-initiation for solitary and eclectic Witches, a handfasting (wedding), or an end of life ceremony. There are as many variations on each of these types of ritual as there are covens and solitary practitioners, and the way a particular Sabbat or Esbat is celebrated may morph and change over the years—in fact, many rituals are made up on the spot.

Furthermore, most covens don't share details of their rituals with non-members. All of this makes it difficult to generalize about the proceedings of ritual in Witchcraft. However, many examples are available in books about the Craft and on Wiccan and other Pagan websites.

At some point during the ritual, magical spells may be worked. Divination may also be employed, particularly at

Samhain, though this might take place after the ritual as well. Once all of the ritual work is completed, the circle is closed, often in a reverse manner to the way it is opened, with the Witch thanking and dismissing the Elements and deities invoked at the start, while walking in the opposite direction. This ensures that the energy raised during ritual has gone completely to its destination in the higher realms, and is not squandered or neglected in the physical plane. It also helps ground the Witch(es) more firmly in the physical plane after reaching intense states of consciousness.

Magical Work

The types, forms, and intentions of magical work occurring during a Wiccan ritual are as varied as every other aspect of Wicca and Witchcraft: It may involve any combination of actions, tools, words, simple or complex spellwork, a tea or brew, chanting and/or movement, candle work, etc.

The options for magical discovery are truly endless. The purpose of the magic can also be anything under the sun—as long as the impact is positive, and does no harm. Many Wiccans choose to work for spiritual as well as material progress, using the Sabbats as opportunities to reflect on their lives at each point in the Wheel and work for balance or any desired change.

However, magical work does not have to be part of Wiccan ritual, and certainly isn't limited to it. Witches will incorporate magical work, as they are able and inclined to do so, into any part of their daily lives.

The tools described in the next section are used in both Wiccan ritual and many other forms of Witchcraft, in the ways and for the purposes that feel appropriate to the Witch(es) who use them.

THE TOOLS

Wiccans and other Witches incorporate a variety of objects into their rituals and magic, many of which are familiar to mainstream culture—you might have heard of some of these tools, and even be able to picture what they look like, from watching television and movies.

However, their presentation in the cinema is often incorrect, with more emphasis placed on entertainment, rather than being portraying the reality of a tool's usage and purpose. For this reason, many of the Wiccan tools are misunderstood.

Let's make this clear: Magic powers don't come streaming in a bolt of light from a Witch's wand, and no one flies on a broom. Both tools are important and sacred to Witchcraft, but in truth, a given Witch may use neither. This is because the power involved in Witchcraft is harnessed by Witches themselves—the tools are merely assistants.

Since the Universe is made of thought, it is ultimately the thought energy behind the actions performed with the tools that causes transformation of reality. Tools can be charged with magical energy, and can be very near and dear to the Witch, but they still need the Witch's intentions to work.

Broom

Perhaps the most common (and commonly misunderstood) symbol of Witches and Witchcraft in popular culture, the broom has been part of Wiccan and other pagan lore around the world for centuries. The sacred broom is not necessarily used in formal Wiccan ritual itself, but is often used to sweep energetic clutter from the ritual space beforehand. The bristles don't actually have to touch the ground, as this kind of cleansing is happening on the psychic and energetic level.

Because it serves as a purifier, it is associated with the element of Water, and is sacred to the Goddess. The broom can also be placed near the entrance to a home to guard against negative or unwanted energy.

The broom can be any size, from miniature "decorative" brooms to larger, full-sized brooms. It might even be a tree-branch used symbolically as a broom. Traditional woods used for sacred brooms include birch, ash, and willow. Many Witches keep hand-made brooms for ritual purposes, but a common household broom can also be dedicated to the work of Witchcraft. No matter what type or material, however, the ritual broom is never used for everyday housecleaning, as this would contaminate the sacred energy it holds for ritual and magical purposes.

Altar

The altar is the sacred place where tools are placed during Wiccan ritual and magic. Traditionally, the altar stands in the center of the circle of energy raised by the participant(s) in the ritual. It may be a table or other object with a flat surface, such as an old chest. It can be square or round, according to preference. Witches may decorate the altar with colored scarves or other material corresponding with the season or the particular purpose of the ritual.

Ideally, the altar is made of wood, such as oak, which is considered to hold significant power, or willow, which is considered sacred to the Goddess. However, it can really be made of any material, as any physical object charged with magical energy will contribute power to the ritual work being enacted.

Witches performing outdoor rituals may use an old tree stump, large stone, or other natural object for an altar, or may use a fire in place of the altar, placing the ritual tools elsewhere in the charged space.

While the altar is usually set up prior to the ritual and taken down afterward, some Witches maintain permanent altars in their homes. These may double as shrines to the

Goddess and God, and can be a place to store the Witch's magical tools.

The tools are deliberately placed in specific patterns on the altar, with intentional regard to the elements and the four directions. For example, tools and symbols associated with the element of Earth may be placed in the North section of the altar, while those associated with water will be placed to the East. Traditional Wiccan practice also often devotes the left side of the altar to representations of the Goddess, while the right side represents the God. While many Witches closely follow established patterns for setting up the altar, others will experiment and use patterns that resonate with their personal relationship with their deities and corresponding tools and symbols.

Wand

Used for millennia in religious and magical rites, the wand has long been associated with Witches and Witchcraft in popular culture, and has also been quite misunderstood.

As with all magical tools, it is not the wand that causes magical transformation, but the Witch, who energetically charges the wand with magical intention. As a shape it takes the form of a line, and so is used to direct energy. It is often used in Wiccan ritual to invoke the Goddess and God, and may be used to draw magical symbols in the air or on the ground. It can also be used to draw the circle within which the ritual or spellwork is performed.

The wand is associated with the element of Air, and is considered sacred to the God.

The wand can be a fairly simple affair, simply cut from a slight branch or twig from a tree (with an attitude of reverence and respect for the tree making the sacrifice). Generally, the wand isn't much longer than the forearm, and can be shorter. Woods traditionally used to make the wand include oak, willow, elder, and hazel. Witches without access to these or other trees might purchase a wooden dowel from a craft or hardware store to decorate and consecrate as a wand. There are also a number of very fancy glass or pewter-based wands decorated with engravings and crystals available at many New Age stores, but wood is the traditional material for Wiccan wands, and it is generally thought that a wand *made* by the Witch who uses it is more effective.

Knife

Also called an *athame*, the ritual knife, like the wand, is a tool that directs energy in ritual, and may also be used to draw the circle before ritual and close the circle afterward.

However, it is more of an energy manipulator or commander, due to its sharp edges, and therefore isn't generally used to invoke deities, as this would be considered forceful, rather than collaborative, in terms of working with divine energy. The athame is also used to draw magical symbols, such as the pentagram, in the air to lend power to ritual and spellwork, and is often employed in rituals that banish and/or release negative energies or influences. This tool is associated with the God, and the element of Fire, as it is an agent that causes change.

The knife is traditionally sharp on both sides, with a black handle which is said to store a small amount of the magical energy raised in rituals for later use. The blade is not generally very long—the length of one's hand, or shorter, is considered ideal.

Some Witches purchase special daggers to serve as their athame, while others will consecrate an ordinary kitchen knife for the purpose. It's considered unwise to use a knife that has been used to cut animal flesh, though any negative energies lingering from such use can be ritually cleansed before "converting" the knife into an athame. Some Witches choose to enhance their energetic relationship with their knife by engraving magical symbols into the handle.

Depending on the tradition, the athame may do double duty as an actual cutting and engraving tool. It may be used to cut herbs, shape a new wand from the branch of a tree, or carve magical symbols into a candle for ritual use. However, many Witches prefer to use a second, white-handled knife (sometimes called a *boline*) for these purposes, keeping the athame for ritual use only.

Cauldron

While the word "cauldron" may bring to mind images of Shakespeare's three witches tossing all kinds of animal parts into a boiling stew for evil purposes, the cauldron is really a symbol of the Goddess and the creative forces of transformation. Cauldrons appear in many ancient Celtic myths in connection with magical occurrences, and continue to influence Witchcraft today. Associated with the element of Water, the cauldron may hold magically charged ingredients for a potion, or may be used to allow spell candles to burn out. It can also be filled with fresh water and used for scrying.

Cast iron is considered the cauldron's ideal material, though other metals are often used. Most rest on three legs, with the opening of the cauldron having a smaller diameter than the widest part of the bowl. Cauldrons can be anywhere from a few inches to a few feet across in diameter, though larger sizes may be considered impractical. While some Witches may actually brew a magical potion right in the cauldron, the practical constraints of lighting a safe indoor fire underneath it tend to limit this use—often, the "brewing" aspect of the magic is symbolic rather than literal.

Cup

Like the cauldron, the cup represents the element of Water and symbolizes the fertility of the Goddess.

An important element of the altar layout during ritual, it may hold water, wine, or possibly a special tea brewed for the magical purpose of the rite. In some rituals it remains empty, as a symbol of readiness to receive new sources of abundance from the Spirit world. Also called the "goblet" or the "chalice" in some traditions, it can be made of any quality substance such as earthenware, crystal, glass, or silver. Solitary Witches may simply dedicate a favorite old family cup, charging it with magical energy and keeping it just for this purpose.

Pentacle

The pentacle is an important symbol-bearer in Witchcraft, normally inscribed with a pentagram, though other magical symbols may be present. The pentagram itself is a five-pointed star, drawn with five straight lines, often encircled, and always having one upward point. Each point is said to represent the elements of Air, Earth, Fire, and Water, with the Fifth Element (Spirit) as the upward point.

As a symbol, it is found in both ancient Eastern and Western cultures and has been used to represent various aspects of human and spiritual concerns. The pentagram is considered to have inherent magical powers, and is often inscribed on objects as well as in the air during rituals, to add strength to the work. It is also considered a sign of protection from negative or harmful energies.

As a bearer of this Earth-related symbol, the pentacle is used to consecrate other tools and objects used in ritual.

Usually a flat, round piece of wood, clay, wax, or silver, it can be any size, though generally is small enough to fit comfortably on the altar with the other tools. The pentacle may be ornately carved and/or set with semiprecious gemstones, or may be a simple design. Witches may also wear a pentacle on a cord or chain during ritual, or even as part of their daily dress, though they may or may not choose to wear it publicly.

Incense

Incense is associated with the element of Air, and, in some traditions, Fire. Smoldering incense is often placed before images of the deities on an altar or a shrine. Many Witches feel that incense is an essential component to successful ritual. This is partly due to the consciousness-altering potential of quality incense, which can facilitate a more focused state of mind when performing magical work.

Smoke from the incense can also provide visions of the deities being invoked in ritual, or other images pertinent to the work being performed. Furthermore, certain herbs, spices, barks, and roots have specific magical qualities, so homemade incense blends can be used to strengthen magical spells.

Whether homemade or store-bought, traditional Wiccan rituals favor raw or granulated incense, which requires charcoal briquettes to burn on, and is usually held in a censer. The censer can be a traditional swinging censer suspended from chains, like those used in the Catholic church, or a more simple construction, depending on whether the incense is moved around during the ritual. Some Witches may let the incense smolder in the cauldron in lieu of a censer.

For Witches who are more sensitive to incense smoke, lighter stick or cone incenses may work better. Some opt for scenting their magical candles with oils instead. Whatever the choice, it's generally agreed that some form of aromatic enhancement is optimal for magical work.

Crystals, Stones, Herbs, and Oils

Perhaps some of the most powerful magical tools are those that come straight from the Earth without much, if any, alteration by human hands. Herbs and semiprecious gemstones have long been known to have healing properties, and are used today in many medicinal systems around the globe. They are also used in Witchcraft, as decorations, offerings, magical enhancements, and even as the focus of some rituals and spells.

Crystals and other stones have their own energies and are considered to be "alive," rather than simply dormant matter. Sensitive people can often feel their energies when holding these stones in their hands or on some other part of their bodies.

Some stones are used for specific purposes in ritual, while others may be more permanent presences on the altar or in other places in a Witch's home. They may range in size from a square half-inch to much larger, and may be polished and/or carved into specific shapes, or left in their raw form. Crystals can be found in many New Age stores as well as online, though they can sometimes still be found in their raw form in certain natural areas.

Crystals may be used to help guard against illness or negative energy, or may aid in divination or other psychic work. They may also be used to lay out the magic circle at the start of ritual. These stones have astrological associations as well as associations with specific gods and goddesses.

Herbs are also associated with specific deities and astrological bodies, and are used in a variety of ways, including magical kitchen edibles, brews and potions, and spell ingredients. Some of the most common kitchen herbs, such as basil, rosemary, and thyme also have magical associations, which doubles their potential for effective magic, as they can be used to make "enchanted" foods.

However, other herbs used in magic are not appropriate to consume, and care should always be taken to know the difference. It is considered ideal for Witches to harvest their own herbs with their ritual knives, whether from a nearby woods or their own kitchen herb "gardens." However, fresh herbs can be found in grocery stores, and many natural food stores also sell a variety of dried herbs in their bulk departments.

Essential oils from plants, seeds, and nuts are used to enhance ritual atmosphere and also as ingredients in spellwork. Oils have metaphysical properties and may be rubbed into spell candles for a specific magical purpose, or used in a skin-safe blend to anoint the body before ritual. Witches often make their own blends of essential oils to strengthen ritual and spellwork. Also used in aromatherapy for healing a number of physical and emotional ailments, essential oils are widely available at natural food stores.

Candles

Last but certainly not least, candles are considered essential to the practice of Witchcraft.

Used as a source of light, as devotional symbols of deity, as a means of communicating with Spirit, and to aid transformation in many spells, candles have a magical way about them as they allow us to work directly with the element of Fire.

Witches work with a variety of candle colors, depending on the deities being represented and/or invoked, as well as any particular magical purposes of a ritual or spell. Candles are a simple and direct way to work with color magic. Colors have their own metaphysical properties, as well as astrological and elemental associations, which will be described in the next section of this guide.

Candles used in the Craft do not need to be fancy or expensive, though some Witches like to have one or more large, long-lasting candles for use on the altar. Candles used for specific spell purposes are usually left to burn out on their own, and so for practical reasons tend to be smaller. Beeswax, tapers, votives and tea light candles can all be used, though many shops sell individual candles sized and colored specifically for spellwork. These tend to be no more than 4 inches tall and less than one half-inch in diameter.

Witches will generally distinguish between candles used for specific ritual purposes and more "multi-purpose" candles used for additional lighting during spellwork (or simply to enhance any evening atmosphere). Candles consecrated for magical use are therefore not used for any other purposes.

Other Tools

Depending on the tradition, the coven, and/or the individual Witch, variations and additions to the tools described above may be used in ritual and spellwork. For example, some Witches use a sword in addition to, or in place of, the ritual knife. However, swords can be impractical for indoor ritual due to their size, and are not as easily obtainable as knives, and so are less commonly used.

A staff is also sometimes used in formal ritual, held by the High Priest or Priestess of a coven. Like the wand, it carries the representations of Air and the God, though in some traditions it represents Fire. It is usually made of wood and may be decorated with magical symbols and/or semiprecious stones.

Many Witches also incorporate divination tools in their ritual practice. These may include runes, tarot cards, a quartz crystal sphere (or "crystal ball") for scrying, or other oracles borrowed from older traditions, such as the I-Ching. Individual items, such as a specific Tarot card or rune, may be incorporated into spells for specific purposes. The crystal sphere is often used on the altar to represent the Goddess. As mentioned previously, divination may take place during a formal ritual, but post-ritual is also considered a good time for this activity, as the Witch is still in a conducive state of mind to communicate with the Spirit world at this time.

Finally, many Witches like to include magically charged jewelry and other elements of "costume" into their practice. Some may simply wear a pentacle on a chain, as mentioned above, while others may don special robes and/or a headpiece encrusted with gemstones to enhance their personal energy during ritual. Witches in some traditions also work naked, which is generally referred to as "sky-clad."

As with any other aspect of Wicca and Witchcraft, there is no set-in-stone way to approach using the tools of ritual and magic. While it's generally considered helpful to use at least a few, if not several, of the tools described above, it is ultimately about the Witch and his or her connection to the specific tools chosen, or the coven members' collective affinities for the specifics of their ritual practice. Those identifying as Wiccans are likely to have some symbolic representation of the Goddess and God at

Sabbat celebrations, and the Goddess at Esbats, but the way this is carried out can vary widely.

While some covens and solitaries may create elaborate rituals using every tool imaginable, others may design very simple affairs involving simply a candle and a crystal. In other words, it's more about using what *feels* inspiring and "in tune," rather than gathering items from a checklist—if it feels out of place, or unpleasantly strange to a particular Witch to purchase and use a cauldron or a censer, or wear special robes, then these items may simply not be necessary or suitable for that person.

This is, of course, a very brief overview of the basic concepts, forms and tools involved in Wicca and other Witchcraft, as opposed to a comprehensive discussion— as is to be expected with such an unusual and widely varying religion as Wicca, other sources will have different things to say about many of the topics discussed here. Readers interested in learning more should consult as many references as they please for a deeper understanding of these beliefs and practices.

For those considering adopting any or all of the practices discussed in this guide, the next section will explore several practical steps one can take on their journey towards practicing Wicca.

NEXT STEPS FOR ASPIRING WICCANS

MOVING FORWARD

Wicca is different from other religions in many respects, not least of which is its lack of centralized structure and official, authoritative texts that spell out specific forms of practice for all to follow.

It also doesn't tend to be evangelistic or seek new members—you won't find many fliers or posters inviting you to the next Sabbat celebration with your local coven.

This leaves it up to individuals interested in the Craft to seek out information and possible connections with others in the Wiccan community. Thankfully, the Internet has made it far easier than it used to be for Wiccans and Witches to find and post information and communicate with each other.

READ AND REACH OUT

The best way to get started is to read widely about Wicca and/or other forms of Paganism. A short list of suggested references is at the end of this guide, and there is an enormous variety of information available in bookstores and online, much of it from venerable and experienced sources. New voices with new visions for the Craft also continue to emerge.

If you read widely enough, you'll encounter conflicting beliefs and advice—and this is a good thing, as it allows you to develop your own personal understanding of the forces and phenomena at work in Wicca and Witchcraft. Follow what resonates with you at the deepest level. If a ritual, spell, a particular philosophy or any other idea doesn't appeal to you, leave it out of your developing practice and keep seeking more information that feels "right." Most Wiccans and Witches will tell you that it takes a long time of study and observation to create an authentic personal relationship with the Craft.

If you're looking to connect with others, depending on where you live there may in fact be a local coven, circle, or other such group that you could join, or at least approach for information and advice. If there is a spiritual or "New Age" store in your area, odds are that someone there will know of any existing groups. You can also check event listings online, in local newspapers, or other community resources. Finally, you can send out an intention to the Universe to help bring the people you're looking for into your life—it may be that a group near you is looking for someone new to join and will look forward to receiving your message!

You can also always start your own "study group" to find like-minded souls who also want to learn more about Wicca, Witchcraft, and/or other forms of Paganism.

COVEN, CIRCLE, SOLITARY, OR ECLECTIC?

For those interested in working with other Wiccans and Witches, covens and circles can be a good way to get solid training and advice from experienced practitioners. The terms "coven" and "circle" *can* be confusing for beginners, as they often seem to be used interchangeably. They are not, however, the same thing.

A *circle* is usually a fairly informal group whose members may get together to discuss and learn about the Craft, and may experiment with different kinds of ritual and spellwork. They may or may not meet for Sabbats and/or Esbats, depending on the collective wishes of the group. Depending on how "open" the group is, there may be many members, some of whom drop in and out as it suits them, or just a few regularly involved friends. The structure of a circle is generally loose and doesn't require official initiation or involve an established hierarchy.

A *coven,* on the other hand, is more structured and usually has one or more established leaders, such as a High Priestess and/or High Priest, especially in what is referred to as "Traditional" Wicca. Covens meet for Sabbats and Esbats and members are expected to attend these gatherings, as the participation of each person is important to the ritual. Initiation is generally required, though it's fairly unlikely that someone brand-new to Wicca will be quickly initiated into a coven, for a few reasons.

One is that covens are generally small groups, with seven being considered an ideal number, and there's a tradition of not going over 13 members—often, if there's enough interest to push a coven past 13, one member will depart to start a new, separate coven. So, depending on how well established a coven is, there may just simply not be any openings.

Secondly, coven members will want potential new initiates to have spent a good deal of time studying before considering inviting them to participate in formal ritual.

Finally, since the bonds formed between coven members are strong and fairly intimate, the question of whether someone's personality and general energy are a good fit is an important one.

For those who don't live near any covens or circles, or who simply prefer not to incorporate a social element into their experience of the Craft, the life of a solitary or eclectic Witch can be just as meaningful and rewarding. Perhaps you'd rather get to know the spiritual and magical dimensions of the Universe on your own for awhile, and then consider reaching out to like-minded others, or perhaps you're just born to be a solo practitioner—and that's perfectly fine! No matter which direction you choose, there's a plethora of informational sources out there to guide you along the way.

The terms "solitary" and "eclectic" may sometimes be used interchangeably, as there can be a lot of overlap, but the distinctions are worth pointing out here.

"*Solitary*" refers to the practice of Wicca or Witchcraft on one's own, without any group experience such as a coven or circle. Wiccans who belong to covens may (and often do) still practice on their own along with their participation in coven work, but a solitary Wiccan or Witch *always* works alone.

A solitary Witch can still intentionally follow what is commonly agreed to be "Traditional" Wicca, such as Gardnerian, British Traditional Wicca, or another "lineage-based" tradition, and those who do so tend to identify as "solitary" rather than "eclectic."

"*Eclectic*" is a description for Witches who don't follow a single, specific tradition and instead borrow and blend ideas, methods, practices, etc. from a variety of sources, and may also (and often do) invent their own. Some covens also consider themselves to be "eclectic," although this tends to irritate members of traditional covens.

It's worth remembering here that even the earliest recognized forms of Traditional Wicca were essentially borrowed, blended, and "invented" themselves.

FINDING YOUR WAY IN

In this section, I want to show you how a newcomer to Wicca may begin to embrace the Wiccan beliefs, way of life, and rituals.

Living the Wheel of the Year

Wicca and Witchcraft are rooted in a relationship with nature and its various expressions in plant and animal life, the elements, and the turning of the seasons. The living, breathing Divine Mind is vibrantly present in nature, perhaps more obviously so than in most of the human-made, modern, "developed world." Those interested in Wicca and Witchcraft will benefit from consciously observing the natural world around them and developing a more intentional relationship with it.

Witches who live in climates with four distinct seasons (Spring, Summer, Autumn and Winter) have an excellent opportunity to closely observe the Wheel of the Year. Sabbats are the best time to note the changes on the Earth and in the sky over the last several weeks, and Esbats also provide occasions for marking the seasons' effects in our everyday lives. The more you pay attention to the space "in between seasons," the more the movement of the Earth becomes apparent—even in Winter.

If you live in a climate with less seasonal variety, or even none at all to speak of, you can still observe the effects of natural forces in subtle ways. The sun still casts different qualities of light throughout the day. The air tends to change just before a rain. Becoming practiced in the habit of observing small details in your natural environment helps cultivate your openness to the unseen energies inherent in all of the Universe.

If you can, go out for walks, hikes, picnics, etc. in places with soil and vegetation. Or go swimming, canoeing, or rock-skipping across a pond. Build a snowman or sculpt your own creation in snow. Do whatever you can to spend some quality time outdoors on a regular basis.

If you live in a very urban environment and have little in the way of access to natural areas, you can still create ways to interact with the underlying forces of the Universe. Parks can be suitable, but so can indoor plants and windowsill gardens. You can grow herbs for magical use and healing as well as cooking. Open a window at sunrise and study whatever you can see of the sky. Stand in the rain for a minute and embrace the feeling of it on your skin. Even nature shows and photographs or art depicting natural scenes can help put you in touch, as well as recordings of nature sounds and meditation music.

When Sabbats come around, make a point of gathering a few of the seasonal gifts of the Earth—flower petals in Spring months, leaves shed from deciduous trees in Autumn, pine needles from evergreens in Winter. Use these in ritual, or simply as decorations on your kitchen table or somewhere else where you'll see them often. As you practice these ways of observing the Wheel of the Year, you'll find your relationship with the seasons (even your least favorite ones) becoming more attuned and rooted in gratitude.

Deities and the Divine

Seeking and attaining a spiritual relationship with the Triple Goddess or Cernunnos or Diana or any other number of deities from around the ancient world can be a very effective way into the Craft, and many people find their experience to be deepened and sharpened through the practice of more traditional, structured forms of Wicca.

But some newcomers to Wicca and Witchcraft are unsure about the notion of "worshipping" deities, and may feel strange about searching for one or more specific gods or goddesses to form relationships or alignments with. Borrowing from older traditions in this respect may not quite feel like an authentic approach to a spiritual search.

It's true that it takes time to find and cultivate an interest in and a relationship with a deity you weren't aware of until recently, and people who were raised in monotheistic religions can struggle even more with integrating the concept of polytheism. But it's also true that you don't absolutely *have* to incorporate a belief in or a relationship with any specific form of the divine. You might just work with the idea of a Goddess and a God, or even less definitively identified energies of the Universe.

Faith and belief are far more often developed and cultivated over time than immediately attained. Make effort to study and seek yours, but go at your own pace, and trust your intuition. No one can tell you you're not a true Wiccan or Witch because your relationship with the divine doesn't match their experience. (Well, some might, but in a religion with so many variations, it's only natural that some will quibble about the details.) There's no intermediary between you and the Universe, and there are as many paths to the Divine as there are people who seek it.

If you do see connecting with deities as a possible part of your path, start doing some research. Read about them—in Wiccan books, in ancient myths, in poetry, in history books. (Watch out for bias in the history books, however—in the Judeo-Christian world, the deities of polytheism often get negatively and erroneously portrayed.) You may discover, as some Witches do, that a deity will actually find you, through images, dreams, seemingly "random" events or coincidences, or in other ways.

Meditation and Visualization

Preparing for ritual and magical work involves accessing a beneficial altered state of mind that allows for both openness and focus. Many traditions practice specific meditation and visualization techniques to strengthen this ability and call on it when needed. You can find information on meditation in Witchcraft or many other spiritual traditions. Seek out different kinds of meditation instruction and practice what works best for you. If nothing else, be sure to set aside time and space for solitude and reflection, preferably every day, but definitely before ritual and spellwork.

EXAMPLE SPELL: A RITUAL OF CELEBRATION AND MAGIC FOR THE AUTUMN EQUINOX

This fairly simple ritual is offered as one example of countless possibilities—I've included it to show you an example of one of the more accessible, and easy-to-perform rituals for the beginner Wiccan.

It's designed for solitary practice, but could certainly be adapted for use with a coven. Like most rituals, it can be tailored to your intuition, preferences, or circumstances. (It can also be replicated for other Sabbats, with changes made to seasonal items, candle colors, etc.) If you don't have everything listed below, you don't have to go out and buy it—you can substitute, simplify, and improvise as you wish. However, you should at least have a candle or two, and some form of recognition of the season to serve as points of focus for your energy—remember, most of the tools are symbolic as the power comes from you, but tools are especially useful for beginners as they give them something tangible to focus and direct their energy onto.

Ready to get started?

Since the Autumn Equinox is a time for celebrating the abundance of the harvest, themes for focus in ritual include gratitude to the Sun for making the harvest possible and to the Earth for yielding abundance to carry through the Winter months.

The balance of equal day and equal night is also good to observe, as is the opportunity to begin a turning inward and looking forward to a more restful time. The end of Summer is also a time when the abundance of the Earth begins to die back in order to make room for new growth in the next cycle. We can use this time to identify what in our lives isn't needed anymore—whether it be too much "stuff," an old habit we've been wanting to break, or anything else that we'd like to release back into the Universe.

As you prepare for the ritual, meditate on these themes and notice what comes to mind. See this opportunity to gain insight into an aspect of your life you may not have been conscious of before.

Recommended Items

- Seasonal representations such as late summer crops, especially corn and squash, apples, seeds, and/or marigolds.

- Candles: 1 black, 1 white, 1 dark green spell candle, and 1 or more others in autumn colors like red, orange, brown, gold, etc.

- Pentacle

- Cup

- Incense and/or oils: frankincense, sandalwood, pine, rosemary, chamomile

- Stones: jade, carnelian, lapis lazuli

- Herbs: sage, hawthorne, cedar

Instructions

Lay out your tools on your altar or ritual space. You can do this in whatever way is most visually pleasing, or you can follow any traditional pattern that appeals to you.

One way is to place the white candle on the left for the Goddess, the black candle on the right for the God, the pentacle to the North and the cup to the West. A candle can be placed in the South—this can be the spell candle, if you're using it, or another candle. Incense or oils can be placed in the East. (If it's not practical to place burning incense right on the altar, you can place it somewhere nearby in the Eastern quarter.) Any stones or representations of the harvest can be placed around the edges of the altar or wherever they seem to "want" to be. Take some time trying out different arrangements. You'll soon get a sense for what looks and feels right for you.

If you want to cast a circle, make sure you have everything you're using for the ritual, and then decide how large your circle will need to be. Using sea salt, sprinkled herbs, candles, or stones, mark out the circle on the ground. Charge the circle with intention for creating a sacred space by slowly walking clockwise around it from the inside. As you walk, "draw" the circle again by pointing with your index finger, visualizing the energetic connection between your body and the circle's edge— remember, you are creating a place of higher, more powerful energy than will exist on the outside of the circle. This is an act that takes practice and learning. It is not strictly necessary, but it is a time-honored part of Wiccan tradition that many find to be integral.

Light the black and white candles and invite the God and Goddess (or the balanced forces of male and female) to be present with you in the celebration. If you wish, call the quarters by turning to stand in each cardinal direction, starting with North and moving clockwise. Verbally recognize each direction by name and its associated element, and ask for its energy to come into your circle. You are already incorporating symbols of the Elements with the pentacle (Earth), the incense or oil (Air), the candles (Fire), and the cup (Water) so you could hold each of these items as you greet the Elements, either instead of calling the quarters or as part of it.

Reflect on the abundance you've experienced in the past season. Identify 7 things you are grateful for and state them aloud. These can be small things or larger ones—whatever you feel truly grateful for at this time. Then, ask for any help you need with establishing balance, maintaining security, and/or letting go of something.

If you're using a spell candle, rub a drop or two of essential oil into it, or just hold it in your hands for a few moments. Visualize yourself feeling secure and grateful for abundance in your life, in good physical health, and emotionally balanced. Out loud, state this vision in whatever way seems most natural to you. You might simply say "I have everything I need. I am in good health. My life is balanced."

Light the green candle as you say the words. Then "seal" the work with a final phrase. Many Witches use one of the following: "So let it be," "So mote it be," "Blessed Be," or "It is done." Whatever you choose, be sure to consciously release your intentions into the higher realms where they can be transformed and manifest. Watch the flame for a few moments, feeling the positive energies raised within you and all around you in the sacred space.

When you're ready, thank the Elements, then the Goddess and God for their presence. Then, close the circle by walking around it counter-clockwise, releasing its energy into the Universe. (Note: Don't leave any candles unattended, but do let the spell candle burn out on its own, if at all possible.)

Over the next few weeks, continue the practice of recognizing abundance and expressing gratitude. You may also notice any seeming imbalances in your life or well-being and decide to do what you can to correct them. If you do so, you will see that the Universe will support you!

WHAT DOES MANIFESTATION LOOK LIKE?

When Witches speak of "manifestation" or "success" in relation to prayer, intention, or spellwork, what do they really mean?

You don't tend to hear fairytale-like stories about enormous, overnight gains in one's quality of life the day after working a spell, though anything can happen if all the right circumstances are in place. What advanced practitioners of the Craft understand is that *practice* is necessary—in the form of time, study, and experiment. One also has to cultivate a mindset that is open to manifestation, to success, and to magical and positive occurrences.

This *can* be a difficult habit to acquire and hold onto, and everyone has their blind spots now and again, but with active practice, the wonders of the Universe begin to unfold more steadily.

Let me show you how.

Once upon a time, a young, aspiring Witch met an older, much more experienced Witch at a folk festival, where they were both camping in the woods. As the festival wound down and everyone was packing up to leave, the two Witches decided to exchange their contact information. Neither had a writing implement, nor could they find any in their tents or packs. Then suddenly, the younger Witch spotted a pencil, "randomly" lying on the forest floor between two trees. "Wow," said the older Witch. "Talk about manifesting!"

The younger Witch was confused. How was this an example of "manifesting"? The pencil hadn't fallen from the sky, or even been suddenly delivered by a passerby out of the blue. Sure, it was a welcome coincidence, but clearly some other person had simply lost a pencil in that spot in the woods, and over a festival weekend, those woods saw their fair share of human artifacts. Furthermore, no spell or incantation had been performed. So how did this pencil count as a manifestation?

The younger Witch was too accustomed to analyzing the possible causes of events to appreciate the synchronicity and Divine timing of this pencil's emergence into her reality. Rather than focusing on the inherent magic of this small event, she instinctively moved to dismiss it in favor of the habitual "rational" thinking instilled in her through cultural conditioning.

This is a challenge faced by many who are new to the Craft, but with persistent willingness to be open to the subtleties of reality underneath our "rational" experience, it becomes easier to recognize all kinds of manifestations, from the "little things" to much larger transformations in our lives.

There are a few key elements in this particular incident that meet the conceptual requirements of manifestation. First, the pencil appeared in the right place at the right time. Second, it fulfilled a specific need that, if met, would be beneficial to both people involved, and would harm no one. Third, it happened in a way that was unexpected, rather than as a result of looking in all the obvious, logical places for something to write with. Manifestation often comes in ways we never could have imagined or planned for.

And as an extra-nice touch, it happened in a natural setting: a forest of old, magnificent trees.

Just as importantly, the pencil was *acknowledged* as a manifestation by the older Witch, who knew from practice how to recognize and appreciate it as such. She also knew that manifestation can happen with or without designated spellwork. Sometimes the Universe simply helps out in moments of need or crisis—these occasions are sometimes called "miracles." Since the older Witch was well grounded in magical principles, she was often able to intend for things immediately and did so habitually, always growing in her ability to connect her personal power with the Divine.

Beyond spellwork, ritual, and intention-setting, the practice of paying attention and acknowledging with gratitude is just as important to successful manifestation. As you start seeing synchronicities in your life, however small, take note and remember them. You may want to record incidents that seem significant in a journal or Book of Shadows. You will find that the more you pay attention to them, the more you will attract positive manifestation in your life.

KEEPING A BOOK OF SHADOWS

The term "Book of Shadows" comes out of the Gardnerian Tradition, but has been widely adopted and adapted by covens, solitaries, and eclectics ever since. Keeping one is a great way for new and experienced Witches alike to deepen their practice of the Craft.

You can think of your Book of Shadows as a kind of journal, specifically for spiritual and/or magical pursuits. The contents of a Book of Shadows are personal and will vary from Witch to Witch. Some keep detailed instructions for rituals and spells, either borrowed from other sources or of their own invention. Some record the results of their magical workings, information about their personal deity alignments, or lists of particular herbs and stones they feel affinity with. Others may free-write about their intentions for a coming ritual or a new season. This can also be a good place to record relevant dreams or other signs and messages that come into your life. It's often illuminating to revisit these at a later date and see underlying connections between seemingly unrelated phenomena!

These are just a few suggestions for digging deeper into the world of Wicca and Witchcraft. As we've seen, it's a wide and richly diverse religion with many possible avenues to follow. No matter what you do, always follow your own intuition when it comes to how, when, and if you want to embark on the path of the Craft.

CONCLUSION

Unlike most other Western religions, Wicca is highly decentralized—there is no official sacred text, no central governing body, and this means there is no one way to practice the religion.

With this in mind, it is very difficult to create a truly encompassing beginner's guide to the topic, simply because different Wiccans will interpret the many facets of the religion differently—in some cases, *very* differently.

In this guide, I have tried to provide an unbiased approach, though undoubtedly my own experiences as a practicing Wiccan might have influenced certain sections of this book. Generally speaking, I have tried to include the most *"popular"* approach to each topic, as this should make the information easier to digest, and you are also more likely to encounter Wiccans with the same set of beliefs—this might make it easier for you to find a local coven with a set of beliefs that truly resonate with you.

However, nothing in this inspiring, fascinating religion is set in stone. Certain sections of this guide might not *feel* right to you, and that's perfectly fine. The great thing about Wicca is that you are free to come up with your own belief system, and as you meet and interact with fellow practitioners, you'll see that some people's interpretations might vary wildly from the views presented in this guide.

There is no right or wrong. As long as you keep the Wiccan principles at heart, and never intentionally seek to harm others, you can practice Wicca in any way you see fit. In fact, I would actively *encourage* you to seek out your own path.

One of the best things about Wicca is that your interpretations, views, and beliefs are highly flexible. When you are just starting out, you are encouraged to read and learn as much as possible, and so your initial beliefs are bound to be shaped by the guides you read.

Over time, when you begin to embrace Wicca in your daily life, you might have certain epiphanies that re-shape your approach to the practicing this religion. What you believe on day one, might be *very* different to your beliefs on day 100, which could be a world apart from your views on day 1,000. It can be a lifelong journey, and even after decades you will still find yourself learning new things. This is one of the many benefits of keeping your own Book of Shadows—you can literally track how your Wiccan journey has evolved over time.

Remember: nobody can tell you how to practice Wicca, and the religion can mean anything you want it to mean to you. While I have presented the information in this guide as "correct", I am in no way suggesting that it is the only way to practice Wicca. If you read other guides, there may be conflicting information. And when you read another guide to the topic, you will likely come across even more conflicting information!

That's just the way Wicca is. Even if you encounter some different opinions—even those completely opposed to what you have read in this guide!—it doesn't mean one guide is right, and another is wrong: it just means the many different authors have interpreted different aspects of the religion differently.

I will leave you with that thought, as it is now time for you to start your own journey, and interpret the information presented to you in your own way. I have included a number of tables of correspondence at the end of this guide, which you should find helpful at some point in time. I have also included a number of suggested sources for further reading, as in the early days it is important for you to absorb as much information as possible on the subject.

I sincerely hoped you enjoyed learning about Wicca with me, as it is a topic close to my heart. It would mean a great deal to me if you continued on your path towards Wicca, but if you choose not to, I hope I have educated you on the belief system of the wonderful people who choose to practice Wicca.

Thank you one more time for reading.

Blessed Be.

TABLES OF CORRESPONDENCE

Tables of correspondence illustrate various qualities and associations of tangible objects like crystals and stones, herbs, and oils, as well as intangible phenomena like colors, months, astrological signs, and even days of the week.

Included here are very brief sample tables of correspondence. You can consult these when exploring options for ritual, spellwork, and other Craft activity. Be sure to research further, however—there are countless tables of correspondence with much more detailed information than is presented in this brief guide.

TABLE ONE: COLORS

Color	Qualities	Magical Uses	Elemental and Other Associations
Red	Passion, courage, strength, intense emotions	Love, physical energy, health, willpower	Fire, South, Mars, Aries
Orange	Energy, attraction, vitality, stimulation	Adaptability to sudden changes, encouragement, power	Mercury, Gemini
Yellow	Intellect, inspiration, imagination, knowledge	Communication, confidence, divination, study	Air, East, Sun, Leo
Green	Abundance, growth, wealth, renewal, balance	Prosperity, employment, fertility, health, good luck	Earth, North, Venus, Libra & Taurus
Blue	Peace, truth, wisdom, protection, patience	Healing, psychic ability, harmony in the home, understanding	Water, West, Jupiter, Sagittarius

Color	Qualities	Magical Uses	Elemental andOther Associations
Indigo	Emotion, fluidity, insight, expressiveness	Meditation, clarity of purpose, spiritual healing, self-mastery	Saturn & Neptune, Capricorn & Pisces
Violet	Spirituality, wisdom, devotion, peace, idealism	Divination, enhancing nurturing qualities, balancing sensitivity	Uranus & Moon, Aquarius & Cancer
Black	Dignity, force, stability, protection	Banishing and releasing negative energies, transformation, enlightenment	Saturn & Pluto, Capricorn & Scorpio
White	Peace, innocence, illumination, purity	Cleansing, clarity, establishing order, spiritual growth and understanding	Spirit (the fifth Element), Mercury & Moon, Virgo

TABLE TWO: CRYSTALS AND GEMSTONES

Crystal	Color(s)	Magical Uses
Amethyst	Violet	Sharpens mental focus and intuition, clears sacred spaces
Bloodstone	Green with flecks of red/gold	Promotes physical healing, fertility, and abundance
Carnelian	Red/orange	Wards off negative energies, inspires courage
Citrine	Yellow	Aids self-confidence, renewal, useful dreams
Hematite	Silver/grey/shiny black	Strengthens willpower and confidence, helps with problem solving
Lapis Lazuli	Blue/dark blue	Helps with altered consciousness, meditation, divination
Moonstone	White/pale blue	Used in Goddess rituals, good for intuition and wisdom
Quartz Crystal	White/clear	Promotes healing, clarity, spiritual development
Rose Quartz	Pink	Promotes emotional healing, love and friendship
Tiger's Eye	Brown/tan/gold with bands of black	Protection, energy

TABLE THREE: HERBS AND ESSENTIAL OILS

Herb	General Magical Uses
Basil	Fosters loving vibrations, protection, wards off negativities in a home
Chamomile	Brings love, healing, relieves stressful situations
Rosemary	Love and lust spells, promotes healthy rest
Thyme	Attracts loyalty, affection, psychic abilities
Valerian	Protection, drives away negativity, purifies sacred space

Essential Oil	General Magical Uses
Bergamot	Promotes energy, success, prosperity
Cinnamon	Increases psychic connections, promotes healing, success, luck
Clove	Protection, courage, banishing negative energies, cleanses auras
Eucalyptus	Healing and purification
Jasmine	Strengthens intuition and inspiration, promotes sensuality and love
Lavender	Healing, cleansing, removing anxiety
Sandalwood	Clears negativity, promotes balanced energy flow

SUGGESTIONS FOR FURTHER READING

Please note that this is a very brief list. Many other interesting and useful resources are available in print and online.

History of Traditional Wicca

Gerald Gardner, *Witchcraft Today* (1955) and *The Meaning of Witchcraft* (1959)

Doreen Valiente, *Where Witchcraft Lives* (1962)

Raymond Buckland, *Witchcraft....The Religion* (1966)

Margot Adler, *Drawing Down the Moon: Witches, Druids, Goddess-Worshippers, and Other Pagans in America* (1979)

Sybil Leek, *The Complete Art of Witchcraft* (1971)

Contemporary Wicca and Witchcraft

Janet and Steward Farrar, *Eight Sabbats for Witches* (1981)

Scott Cunningham, *Wicca: A Guide for the Solitary Practitioner* (1989)

Ellen Dugan, *Natural Witchery: Intuitive, Personal & Practical Magick* (2007)

Laurie Cabot with Tom Cowan, *Power of the Witch: The Earth, the Moon, and the Magical Path to Enlightenment* (1990)

D.J. Conway, *Celtic Magic* (1990)

Science and Magic

Itzhak Bentov, *Stalking the Wild Pendulum: On the Mechanics of Consciousness* (1977)

John C. Briggs and F. David Peat, *Looking Glass Universe: The Emerging Science of Wholeness* (1986)

F. David Peat, *Synchronicity: The Bridge between Matter and Mind* (1987)

Fritjof Capra, *The Tao of Physics: An Exploration of the Parallels Between Modern Physics and Eastern Mysticism* (2010)

DID YOU ENJOY *WICCA FOR BEGINNERS?*

Again let me thank you for purchasing and reading my guide. There are a number of great books on the topic, so I really appreciate you choosing this one.

If you enjoyed the book, I'd like to ask for a small favor in return. If possible, I'd love for you to take a couple of minutes to leave a review for this book on Amazon.

Your feedback will help me to make improvements to this guide, as well as writing books on other topics that might be of interest to you. Hopefully this will allow me to create even better guides in the future!

OTHER BOOKS BY LISA CHAMBERLAIN

Wicca for Beginners: A Guide to Wiccan Beliefs, Rituals, Magic, and Witchcraft

Wicca Herbal Magic: A Beginner's Guide to Practicing Wiccan Herbal Magic, with Simple Herb Spells

Wicca Book of Spells: A Book of Shadows for Wiccans, Witches, and Other Practitioners of Magic

Wicca Book of Herbal Spells: A Book of Shadows for Wiccans, Witches, and Other Practitioners of Herbal Magic

Wicca Candle Magic: A Beginner's Guide to Practicing Wiccan Candle Magic, with Simple Candle Spells

Wicca Crystal Magic: A Beginner's Guide to Practicing Wiccan Crystal Magic, with Simple Crystal Spells

Wicca Moon Magic: A Wiccan's Guide and Grimoire for Working Magic with Lunar Energies

Wicca Essential Oils Magic: A Beginner's Guide to Working with Magical Oils, with Simple Recipes and Spells

Wicca Elemental Magic: A Guide to the Elements, Witchcraft, and Magical Spells

Tarot for Beginners: A Guide to Psychic Tarot Reading, Real Tarot Card Meanings, and Simple Tarot Spreads

Wicca Magical Deities: A Guide to the Wiccan God and Goddess, and Choosing a Deity to Work Magic With

Wicca Wheel of the Year Magic: A Beginner's Guide to the Sabbats, with History, Symbolism, Celebration Ideas, and Dedicated Sabbat Spells

Wicca Living a Magical Life: A Guide to Initiation and Navigating Your Journey in the Craft

Magic and the Law of Attraction: A Witch's Guide to the Magic of Intention, Raising Your Frequency, and Building Your Reality

Wicca Altar and Tools: A Beginner's Guide to Wiccan Altars, Tools for Spellwork, and Casting the Circle

Wicca Finding Your Path: A Beginner's Guide to Wiccan Traditions, Solitary Practitioners, Eclectic Witches, Covens, and Circles

Wicca Book of Shadows: A Beginner's Guide to Keeping Your Own Book of Shadows and the History of Grimoires

Modern Witchcraft and Magic for Beginners: A Guide to Traditional and Contemporary Paths, with Magical Techniques for the Beginner Witch

FREE GIFT REMINDER

I'd hate for you to miss out, so here is one final reminder of the free, downloadable eBook that I'm giving away to my readers.

Wicca: Little Book of Wiccan Spells is ideal for any Wiccans who want to start practicing magic. It contains a collection of ten spells that I have deemed suitable for beginners.

You can download it by visiting:

www.wiccaliving.com/bonus

I hope you enjoy it.

Made in the USA
Middletown, DE
30 June 2018